*Second-language
learning and teaching*

SECOND-LANGUAGE
LEARNING AND TEACHING

D. A. Wilkins
Department of Linguistic Science
University of Reading

Edward Arnold

© D. A. Wilkins 1974
First published 1974
by Edward Arnold (Publishers) Ltd
25 Hill Street, London W1X 8LL

ISBN: 0 7131 5758 5 Boards Edition
       0 7131 5759 3 Paper Edition

Printed in Great Britain by
Billing & Sons Ltd
Guildford and London

Contents

Acknowledgements

Although this book expresses a personal view of language teaching, I have been able to benefit from suggestions made by a number of colleagues in the University of Reading and elsewhere. Former students have also contributed much through the opinions they have expressed in our discussions of the issues raised here. Those examples which are not my own have been drawn from R. H. Robins, *General linguistics: an introductory survey* (Longman, 1971) and J. Lyons, *Introduction to theoretical linguistics* (Cambridge University Press, 1968). I have borrowed the example on page 19 from Svante Hjelmström.

Note on further reading

If the reader should be interested in exploring further any of the areas discussed in this book, the following titles are recommended.

On language:
  D. Bolinger, *Aspects of language* (New York, Harcourt, Brace, Jovanovich, 1968)

On language acquisition:
  P. S. Dale, *Language development* (New York, Holt, Rinehart & Winston, 1972)

On language teaching:
  W. M. Rivers, *Teaching foreign language skills* (Chicago, University of Chicago Press, 1968)

Prologue

It is my belief that there is no single, 'best' way of teaching foreign languages. We can neither select one of the number of well-publicized methods that is proposed to us, nor, by taking account of the undoubted weaknesses of each of them, can we arrive at a more satisfactory alternative. Language learning does not have to proceed by the same path whatever the objectives and circumstances of learning. The readiness of some methodologists to condemn certain kinds of language teaching and to promote others, and their desire to impose unique solutions regardless of the aims of learning and the conditions under which it is to take place, is in my view the result of far too narrow a conception of the principles that govern language learning. Language teaching is a pragmatic business and we should judge it accordingly. What works is good; what does not work is bad. Unfortunately, it is not at all easy to decide what does and what does not work, but at least we should be on our guard against importing a ready-made set of principles against which any piece of language teaching can be judged whatever the teaching situation. We know that in some cases, with certain pupils and with certain teachers, methods that we commonly castigate can be successful and conversely that methods that find general favour can fail. The reason is that the principles that govern language learning are sufficiently general to permit the same goals to be reached by methods and techniques that vary considerably in their details and to necessitate different approaches for different goals.

The aim of this book is to try to establish what these general principles are by looking first at the nature of the subject-matter, language, then at what is known about the learning of languages and finally at the way in which external factors can affect learning.

From this I attempt to deduce what the necessary and sufficient conditions for language learning are and to suggest what the fundamental characteristics of successful language teaching are. As I have said, I believe the principles of sound language teaching to be very general. I am therefore not concerned with and do not discuss specific teaching techniques. Different techniques can be used within the principles that I put forward, and although the contribution that any technique makes to language learning has to be assessed in the light of what is known about language in general, the specific language being taught and the facts of learning, no technique is actually excluded as a matter of principle.

By *language teaching* I mean both second- and foreign-language teaching and except where I have limited these two terms to their more technical use (and such instances are, I hope, self-evident), I intend them to be understood as synonymous. In the absence of a term which covers both kinds of learning, I have used *second-language learning* in the title, but intend it to include *foreign-language learning*.

I address myself to all who have an interest in language teaching, but one eye is firmly on language teachers in training. I assume no previous knowledge of linguistics or psychology but the book will be read with greatest understanding by those with a knowledge of recent developments in language teaching. The principles that I propose are general, but, I hope, not vague. They certainly have very practical implications and I hope that these are clear.

1 The nature of language

1.1 The versatility of language

Language is a means of communication. Although not the only form of communication among human beings, it is certainly the most important. We can communicate in ways that do not involve language, as when advertisers provide powerful visual associations for their products or when we use bodily movements, frowns, shrugs, headshakings and so on. Some apparently non-linguistic means of communication are no more than symbol systems for language itself, for example morse-code, shorthand and sign language. The symbols of these systems refer to units of language, and it is these latter which are given a semantic interpretation. Human language differs from animal 'language' not only in the unique way in which it exploits sound, the substance of expression, but also in the enormous subtlety of variation in content that its formal structure permits. Our entire elaborate social structure is mediated through language, and it is inconceivable that we could have constructed so complex a social interaction if we had not had spoken and, latterly, written language at our disposal. Language is central to human experience and if we are to understand the process by which men communicate with one another, we must look closely at the human capacity for language and at the particular qualities of language which enable it to play so powerful a role within us and between us.

We might well begin by considering just how successfully we do communicate through language. We find in fact that we have a remarkable versatility. We never know what we are going to need to communicate and yet when the time comes, as mature speakers of the language, provided the necessary knowledge and experience itself is not lacking, we have no difficulty in expressing whatever it may be we have the need to express. Whether we are involved in day-to-day interaction with members of our family, in complex explanations of unforeseen events, in emotional reactions to unexpected happenings, in the familiar or the unfamiliar alike, we can quite unconsciously apply our knowledge of language to meeting the demands of what we need to say or write. Nor is this in some way a feat of memory. We do not know how to express ourselves because we have often had to do so in the same or similar ways in the past. It is very rare that what we wish to express now is exactly the same as something we have wanted to say previously. There is usually some difference of emphasis, of conviction or of situation at the very least. In other words, the demands that we want to place on language are virtually limitless.

It is perhaps the most important characteristic of language that it is formed in a way that enables it to meet these demands. Just as life itself places us in situations that are never twice quite the same, so language allows us continually to express novel propositions. Our faculty of language is a faculty of linguistic creativity. Most of the sentences we utter have never been constructed by us previously and many, indeed, have never been constructed by anyone else either. There is literally no limit to the number of sentences that we can create in English, for example. This is not, as one might first suppose, because the vocabulary of the language is very large and is constantly being added to. Even if at any one moment there were a limit to the number of words in the language, there would still be no limit to the number of sentences.

The explanation of this significant fact may seem rather technical and possibly, in a sense, unrealistic. It lies in the fact that sentences may always contain other sentences. No more need really be said, but to make it quite explicit, this means that the sentence which is already within (or conjoined to) another sentence may itself contain a sentence. This embedded sentence need not appear as a full sentence. It may be reduced to an adjective, a phrase or a relative clause, for example. But in principle it is never possible to say:

'There are already so many adjectives before that noun that it is impossible to add one more.' I said that this explanation may seem rather unrealistic. There are good reasons why we might, in the real world, wish to limit the length of any utterance. Our hearers might be less tolerant of this infinite capability than the grammar of the language would be. However, it remains the case that the grammar alone would not place any such restriction on our utterances. We could prolong the uttering of a sentence that remained grammatical long after the audience had removed itself from our presence.

Fortunately, although the number of potential sentences in any language is infinite, the means by which they are constructed are limited. Once it is accepted that sentences can be embedded within sentences and that there is no restriction to the number of times that this may be done, it is possible to understand how an infinite product may be derived from finite means. Although, therefore, in our everyday use of language we continually need to express new statements and, consequently, must have the linguistic ability to do this, the rules we use are not infinite in number.

The ultimate aim in learning a second language must generally be to achieve the same flexibility, the same linguistic creativity that the native speaker possesses. This is not to say that we can expect the same degree of language proficiency, but that the criterion of our success as teachers is not whether our pupils can remember so many sentences, so many phrases, so many words that they have been taught, but whether they can construct new utterances in the language. There are occasions when a lower objective than this might be set, but, in that case, it is not truly language that is being learned.

It follows that the principal task in the learning of a second language is the mastering of the finite system by which linguistic creativity is achieved. A descriptive Grammar of the language conventionally attempts to set out for us the limited rules governing the construction of sentences. The more intensive study of language of recent decades has led us to regard most older Grammars as unduly narrow in scope, but, although there is now more to be said about language, the type of information that Grammars have always provided will continue to occupy a central position in any more comprehensive account of language. Grammars may also have been too limited in outlook, in that grammarians have sometimes judged it to be their role to act as arbiters of what should be acceptable usage. Few grammarians now would attempt to use their authority to resist linguistic innovations or to label the normal speech of some social groups as 'incorrect' or 'ungrammatical'. It is the descriptive as opposed to the prescriptive function of a Grammar that contributes to our understanding of language.

How is a language organized to meet the demands that the individual's desire to communicate will place upon it? As well as possessing a set of grammatical rules through which linguistic creativity is achieved, language contains a system of symbols by means of which we can refer to entities in the physical world and can express more abstract concepts. These symbols constitute the vocabulary or lexicon of the language and they are listed in a dictionary. The way in which the grammatical system is applied in the actual process of communication depends on features of the individuals involved, the setting in which the communication takes place and the purposes of the users. These factors can consistently influence the speaker's choice of linguistic forms. Finally, there are rules governing the way in which language is expressed physically, either as sound or as visible shapes on paper. Except for intonation the phonic and graphic substance of language contributes only indirectly to meaning. The native speaker's linguistic competence is made up of a knowledge of all these aspects of language; but in considering in more detail the task that faces the language learner, let us look first at the role and nature of grammatical systems.

1.2 Grammatical meaning and grammatical form

When we use language, among other things, we express our ideas about the world that surrounds us. We talk about the things we see happening; who or what is responsible for the events that take place; who or what is affected by them. We refer to the objects of the physical world and to their qualities. We can report the activities that are carried out and the manner in which they are done. We can express the way in which events are related in time to one another and to the moment of speech. Events occur in a spatial as well as a temporal dimension, so we need to be able to describe locations, directions and movements. At the same time as we are constructing a message to convey these and other kinds of meaning, we express our attitudes about the truth and reliability of the report we are making, whether it is certain or uncertain, desired or doubted.

Languages possess grammatical systems not, as some learners might be inclined to think, simply to make the learning of the language more difficult, but to express the kinds of meanings that we have just mentioned, which are themselves the whole purpose of communication. The grammatical devices of a language are not to be learned as an end in themselves. It is the capacity to express meaning that is the end. The grammatical system provides the necessary means.

The terms in which these meanings have been described have been deliberately vague. This is because, although it may be true to say that grammatical systems express the same *kinds* of meaning, in *detail* grammatical meaning varies considerably from language to language in just the same way as the grammatical devices themselves may differ quite radically. Grammatical form and grammatical meaning are the two sides of the same coin. Detailed examination of grammatical meaning is impossible without reference to the forms that carry the meaning, and the formal systems cannot be looked at in isolation from the meanings they convey. In the following discussion of the kinds of grammatical units and categories that languages commonly possess, the fact that formal systems are taken as the starting-point should not be taken to imply that grammatical form has priority over grammatical meaning. In learning, mastery of the forms would be valueless without equal mastery of the meanings they convey.

Making a description of the system that exists in a language to express grammatical meaning is essentially a matter of stating what happens to words when they are placed together in sentences. It is common for such statements to be divided into two parts: statements about the *morphology* or the internal structure of words in the language, and statements about the *syntax* or the relations between words in the sentence. However, the distinction between the two is by no means a clear one. They may have very similar functions, in that the grammatical meaning that is conveyed by morphological devices in one language may be marked syntactically in another. The Finnish case system expresses meanings that in English require a prepositional phrase. For example, the Elative form of the noun *talo*, 'house', is *talosta*, which would be rendered as 'out of the house' in English. There is frequently also interaction between morphology and syntax. The exact morphological form of a past tense verb in a Russian sentence depends on the gender and number of the noun (Subject) with which it is syntactically associated. We tend to assume that the major burden of learning a foreign language is in mastering the inflectional characteristics of the language, but, in fact, the problems posed by rules of syntax are not necessarily any smaller.

In order to give a satisfactory account of the structure of a language, it is necessary to recognize that it can be split into units of different sizes. We have already made this assumption in talking about *words* and *sentences*. The existence of these units is not self-evident in the stream of speech. They are not handily marked off by pauses as they are separated by spaces in written language. None the less, we could not make an adequate description of a language without them. The word is the smallest unit capable of relatively independent occurrence and the sentence the largest unit for which we can offer a more or less exhaustive analysis. Words themselves may be made up of smaller units which will recur in different combinations. *Rapidly* is made up of *rapid*, which occurs independently as an adjective, and *-ly*, which is also found in *happily*. *Walked* is made up of *walk*, which occurs in *walking* and *-ed* which recurs in *talked*. Languages like Turkish are said to be *agglutinative* because of the characteristic way in which suffixes can be progressively added to a stem. The word *odalarimdan* is made up of *oda* (room), *-lar* (plural), *-im* (first person), *-dan* (ablative case). Words also combine to form larger units within the sentence, traditionally labelled *phrases* and *clauses*. Grammatical relations between different sentences also exist, although it is not possible to identify a unit such as a *paragraph* because it would not be possible to state its structure in exhaustive terms.

We can account for the behaviour of words in sentences by recognizing that they belong to *classes*, the members of which have similar formal and, less certainly, semantic characteristics. *Nouns* are words which perform similar functions in sentences, for example, acting as Subjects of verbs. *Adjectives* are words which occur as modifiers of nouns and as predicates. Other classes of words that might be established in this way are *verbs*, *prepositions* and *adverbs*. These obviously resemble the traditional *parts of speech*, but the resemblance can be deceptive. The traditional class of adverbs in English, for example, contains items such as *very*, *never* and *slowly*, which have little in common grammatically. An adequate linguistic description would distinguish between them. Speakers of European languages tend to make assumptions about the universality of these classes, but that is because they themselves speak languages that are closely related to one another. If one looks further afield, one finds different numbers and types of word-classes and differing lexical memberships of those classes. The greater the difference between the unit and class structure of the learner's mother-tongue and the second language, the greater the difficulty he is likely to have in acquiring the latter. We should not let the similarity of many European languages in these respects deceive us into thinking that they are relatively unimportant in language learning.

Central to the grammar of any language are the grammatical categories that it exploits. There is a very wide variety of grammatical devices which are familiar to us in one or another of the world's languages. One language will contain only certain of the grammatical categories, and even where the same category is found in two languages it can be realized in radically different ways. Therein lies the problem for the language learner. *Case* is an inflectional category of nouns, adjectives and pronouns. There are languages like French, which has no case system in nouns and adjectives, others like Russian, which has six cases in the noun and adjective and others like Finnish, which has fifteen cases in the noun. Case expresses the relations between nouns and other items in the sentence, particularly verbs and other nouns. These are the relations which tell us such things as *who* (or *what*) did *what* to *whom*, with *what result* and by *what means*. The labels given to cases sometimes give a fairly transparent indication of their syntactic meaning. For an English speaker this would be true for *instrumental* case, for example, whereas the meaning of labels like *nominative* and *genitive* is only apparent to someone who is familiar with a supposedly universal grammatical terminology. Given that each case is likely to represent a distinct syntactic function and that there is so much variation in the number of cases found in different languages, there is obviously much more for the learner in mastering case than simply overcoming the difficulties posed by its morphological forms. Even where languages have an identical number of cases, they will not necessarily express the same syntactic relations.

Number and *gender* are categories which often interact significantly with case. Number is an important semantic category as well as being a formal grammatical category, and where a language possesses the grammatical category of number, its semantic significance is usually self-evident. There are languages which do not mark number at all as an inflectional characteristic of nouns, adjectives or verbs, although this is not to say that they do not possess the means of conveying semantic number. The most common distinction is between singular and plural, but other languages possess three or even four grammatical numbers. Fijian, for example, has singular, dual, trial and plural. Since we use labels like *masculine, feminine* and *neuter* to refer to the different possibilities within the category of gender, it would appear that this too is a category for which it is easy to supply a semantic interpretation. In fact gender systems often have little to do with the semantic division between male, female and neuter. Male beings may be grammatically feminine or neuter. In French *la sentinelle* (sentry) is feminine but normally male, and the grammatical system requires that inanimate nouns no less than animate nouns should be assigned to one of the two genders. The direct semantic vacuousness of some gender systems is perhaps indicated by the fact that although gender is a feature of nouns, there are examples, of which French is one, of languages where the noun itself is not marked for gender, although other words which are in concord with the noun (adjectives and articles in the case of French) do show it. In cases like this the role of gender is to express syntactic relations in much the same way as case and word-order may.

As explained below, it also contributes to the redundancy of language.

One type of meaning expressed by grammatical systems is *deictic* meaning. By *deixis* is meant the relation between a sentence or part of a sentence and the context in which it is uttered. By context here is meant both linguistic and non-linguistic context. One type of deixis is *person deixis* and this is normally realized through article and pronoun systems. In the non-linguistic context pronouns like *he, she, this* and *that* are used to indicate people and objects that can be seen in the context of utterance. They may also be used for reference within the text. Depending on the language the definite articles and demonstrative pronouns, for example, may be used to show that the noun with which they are associated has previously been mentioned in the linguistic context. Personal pronouns can be used as substitutes for nouns which have already occurred. Article and pronoun systems vary from language to language, both in the number of forms and the way in which they are realized. In Macedonian, for example, there are three forms of definite article (excluding variation for number and gender) and they occur as suffixes to the noun.

Another type of deixis is *place deixis*. Through adverbs, events can be oriented to the place of utterance. *Here* and *there* can refer to either the physical or the linguistic context. Academic authors frequently relate a point being made to some other part of their text by use of *above* and *below*. A sentence like *Put it there* contains examples of both person and place deixis. Without knowing more of the circumstances of use, we cannot say whether the pronoun in this sentence refers to the linguistic or the non-linguistic context.

Time deixis can also be expressed adverbially. *Now* and *then* would be examples from English. However, more significantly, it is also possible to regard *tense* systems as essentially deictic. Tense is a morphological characteristic of verbs. When we choose a tense, we place the reported event or proposition in time by indicating that the process involved preceded, succeeded or was simultaneous with the moment of speech. Equally, we can use the tense system to relate one event to another that has been previously mentioned. It is a mistake, however, to think that tenses indicate only features of time or that time itself is marked only in verbal systems. There are many languages from which the category of tense is wholly missing, but this does not mean that concepts of time cannot be expressed in them. In a language like Thai, aspects of time are indicated by the use of adverbs and particles rather than inflection of the verb. It is also the case that those languages that do possess the category of tense rarely make a neat division into past, present and future time grammatically. It is also possible through tense to indicate the character of an event, or, at least, the speaker's view of its character in respect of its duration, completeness, repetitiveness and so on. Slavonic languages possess verbal forms whose function it is to express this kind of meaning. Events are seen by the speaker as complete or incomplete and are encoded accordingly in the *perfective* or the *imperfective aspect*.

Aspect in effect involves a quantification of events parallelling the quantification of things which is a feature of nouns in some languages. English distinguishes between countable nouns like *book* and uncountable nouns like *milk*. With a few exceptions, uncountable nouns have no plurals and, although countability is not otherwise marked in the noun itself, different quantifiers are used with each category of nouns.

With some languages it is necessary to recognize a further verbal category of *mood*. Latin has three moods, indicative, subjunctive and imperative. In English the subjunctive is little used, but on the other hand English possesses a grammatical category of modal verbs which have semantic similarities with subjunctives in other languages. It is not possible to be very precise about what is conveyed by modal systems. In general, while the indicative asserts the truth of the sentence, use of a modal form suggests that the content of a statement is not yet actualized or is uncertainly realized. It can therefore be used to express obligations, doubts, possibilities, wishes and so on.

An important syntactic category is *word-order*. Languages may have relatively free or relatively fixed word-order. If the word-orders are fixed they may none the less follow different rules in different languages. Where in one language the Object may precede the verb, in another it may follow it. Not only is it the sequence of items that is important, their relative contiguity may also determine their exact relationship. Word-order is used much as case is to mark the fundamental syntactic relations between items within the sentence. Some languages possess a further category of *voice*— active, middle, passive voice—which enables the same syntactic relations to be expressed in different sentence forms so as to give differing degrees of emphasis and prominence to the various parts of the sentence.

It is often quite wrongly assumed that there is little more to syntax than questions of word-order, but the whole question of the way in which relatively simple linguistic forms combine to form more complex structures is a matter of syntax. This in turn accounts for our linguistic creativity. As was mentioned above, sentences can be combined to form co-ordinate structures and can also be embedded within one another. An embedded sentence may be in the form of what is traditionally called a subordinate clause, but modern linguists regard all more complex structures, from relative clauses, to phrases containing non-finite verbs, to the simple modification of a noun by an adjective, as the result of sentence-embeddings. The number of embedding processes that any language possesses will be vast and the rules that govern what happens to the forms that are combined in this way—what combinations are permitted and what are not, what forms must be obligatorily included or excluded—are complex and present a considerable problem to the language learner.

He will meet a further problem in the fact that grammatical meaning is not always made fully explicit. The grammatical form of a sentence may not provide all that is necessary for an understanding of the grammatical meaning. This results in potential ambiguity and requires the hearer to bring more to the task of interpreting an utterance than the simple capacity to identify the grammatical markers that are actually expressed. For example, in a sentence like

The case is too heavy to lift

the infinitive has a passive meaning and could be replaced by *to be lifted*. A *hand-towel* is a towel for drying your hands, but a *bath-towel* is not a towel for drying the bath. In

I advised him to drive more slowly

drive is future in relation to *advise*, whereas in

> I knew him to drive very fast

drive is timeless in relation to *knew*. Superficially these latter two sentences have the same structure and, one might think, the elements in the sentence should relate to one another in the same way. Part of what the native speaker knows about his language is that grammatical meaning does not always have overt expression in one or other of the grammatical categories that we have been sketching above. The language learner must ultimately be able to recognize what is covertly present in the form of a sentence.

There are also certain general facts about grammatical systems which are important for the language learner, some of which have been implicit in the preceding discussion. In the first place, languages vary enormously in the devices they use to express the different kinds of grammatical meaning. We have seen that where English uses word-order to express basic syntactic relations, Russian uses a fairly elaborate case system, and that some languages have simple verb forms with no tenses. Number is not always expressed by means of the process of suffixation with which we are familiar in many European languages. In Malay, if no quantifier or numeral is used, plurality is indicated by repetition of the noun in a process known as *reduplication:* 'car' is *kereta;* 'cars' is *kereta-kereta.*

Secondly, although in some degree grammatical meanings reflect 'facts of the world'—this would be true of some of the more fundamental syntactic relations, for example—it is perhaps better to emphasize the extent to which grammatical meanings vary from language to language. Languages frequently lack grammatical systems which are semantically equivalent. There is no grammatical system, verbal or otherwise, in French or German which is equivalent to aspect in Russian. The choice between perfective and imperfective is obligatory in Russian. The French grammatical system does not impose such a choice, although if the speaker wishes to state the completeness or the incompleteness of an event he can do it by other means. The English learner of Finnish will be quite un-accustomed to making the seemingly complex spatial and directional distinctions that are needed for mastery of the case system. Not only does the Finnish noun have a Nominative and a Genitive case, it also possesses such forms as an Essive (expressing a state), a Translative (state resulting from a change), a Partitive (some of . . .), an Inessive (in the . . .), an Elative (out of the . . .), an Ilative (into the . . .). In all there are fifteen forms in the Finnish case system. Few languages have a verbal category that links past events with present significance in the way that the English present perfect does. To a certain extent we are drilled in our perception of events by the semantic nature of the grammatical categories that are provided by our native language. Learning another language means learning to see the world in the way that speakers of that language see it, and this can be a difficult though certainly not impossible task.

This may seem to imply that within any language there is a standard way of perceiving and reporting events; but this too is an oversimplification which can have some significance for language teaching. In fact the speaker has choices which enable him to characterize events in the way in which he personally perceives them. Many of our linguistic choices are not objectively determined, in the sense that it is not entirely the nature of the events that decides how a message about those events is formed.

> Few Englishmen speak foreign languages well
> A few Englishmen speak foreign languages well

The difference between the above sentences lies not in the number of Englishmen involved—it could well be identical in each case—but in whether the speaker has chosen to characterize the facts negatively or positively. In the same way the choice between use of the past tense and the present perfect in English does not depend on the time at which the reported event took place, but on whether or not the speaker wishes to express a link between the past event and present time. This means that linguistic meanings can never be made entirely clear by manipulation of the non-linguistic context in which the forms occur, although this is a favourite technique for teaching the meaning of grammatical forms.

They cannot be made entirely clear either unless linguistic forms are related to one another. The view that language is structured means that any single linguistic form occupies a point in a network of relationships with other linguistic forms. The linguistic meaning of that form is the product of those relationships. The forms cannot be fully learned if they are isolated from one another. They must be placed within the linguistic systems in which they operate. The learner of German will have little understanding of the personal pronoun *es* if it has not yet been contrasted with *er* and *sie*. If the learner is English he might be told that *es* means *it*, just as *er* means *he* and *sie* means *she*, but even the apparent parallelism of this three-term distinction within the larger pronoun system is most misleading. The choice between the German pronouns is one of gender. That between the English pronouns is one of sex. So, not only must *es* be understood in relation to other pronouns, the pronouns themselves must be related to features of the noun system. This is an excellent demonstration of how there is more to language learning than mastering the forms through which the morphological systems are realized. These German forms are not in themselves difficult to learn, but it is impossible to use them accurately unless it is known how they function in fully grammatical sentences or larger stretches of language. Morphology cannot be divorced from syntax in language learning.

1.2.1 Redundancy

In this brief survey of grammatical categories we have seen enough for it to be evident that grammatical systems contribute a great deal to the communicative content of utterances. For us to be able to put an accurate interpretation on an utterance, we need to be able to recognize the grammatical systems that are operating. It is, however, a fact that even where there is grammatical inaccuracy, communication can still take place successfully. The reason for this is to be found in the natural *redundancy* of language. We have seen that there are often several different ways in which grammatical meaning might be expressed. So far we have emphasized the fact that different languages often use different devices, but it is also true that one language may use several grammatical means simultaneously to express the same meaning. This is what is meant by redundancy. The relation of Subject to verb might be evident from the occurrence of the Subject noun in the nominative case, but it can be reinforced, in those languages which possess these devices, by gender, number and person concord between the noun and the verb and perhaps by word-order as well. Past time might be marked both in the verb and in an adverbial expression. Location might be indicated both by the selection of a preposition and by the case of the noun associated with the preposition. The relation between an adjective and the noun it modifies might be marked by the placement of the adjective next to the noun, but also by concord between the adjective and the noun for case, gender and number. It is this apparent over-provision of information that is called redundancy, and it is a feature equally of the lexical and phonological systems of language. It frequently happens that contextual information also duplicates what is provided linguistically.

Because of the natural redundancy of language it does not often happen that the occurrence of a grammatical, lexical or phonological error causes a major breakdown of communication. Even a speaker who has made a mistake is often understood. One could imagine a far more economical, 'ideal' language, but any error in encoding a message in such a language would result in a loss of information. The fact that all human languages are redundant in this sense suggests that redundancy is necessary for the effective communication of messages. This is probably because spoken language is often produced under far from ideal conditions. Redundancy can hardly be less important for the foreigner than it is for the native speaker of the language, and it is for this reason that the language learner should continue to work towards accuracy and correctness in his use of the target language. The individual mistake is significant, not because in itself it will interfere with communication, but because it reduces the overall redundancy of the pupil's language. If non-native speakers are to communicate with anything like the effec-tiveness of native speakers they must eliminate as far as possible accentual features of pronunciation, faults of grammatical and lexical selection and grammatical malformations. This does not imply that the teacher should always insist upon the production of correct forms, nor that he should never let mistakes pass uncorrected. But it is reasonable to set up accuracy alongside spontaneity, fluency, and appropriacy as the ultimate targets in language learning.

1.3 Sociolinguistic variation

Although grammar is central to the study of language, it does not include all that is needed for the successful communication of meaning. Language is produced in a definable context, and it is important that the language forms used should be appropriate to the context. Any speaker automatically selects, from what the language permits, the vocabulary and grammar which are suited to his *topic*. But this is obvious and not particularly significant. More to the point is that there are various dimensions to the social context of utterance and that these dimensions impose restraints on our choice of language. The speaker is not an entirely free agent. He cannot select at will from the grammatical and lexical store of the language. At least, if he does, he risks conveying to his hearer meanings other than those he intended.

There are a number of important social dimensions. We make significant linguistic choices according to whether we are expressing ourselves in *speech* or *writing*. To speak as we write is to risk sounding like a talking book. Some vocabulary items, not only colloquialisms, are preferred in speech over alternatives which are found in written language. There are similarly grammatical structures which are avoided in speech and others which are used frequently in speech but scarcely at all in writing. Spoken utterances, especially in conversation, are sometimes not wholly grammatical. Parts of sentences are elided. Others are quite simply incomplete. Sometimes a sentence changes course in mid-utterance. Many of these features of spoken language can be seen in the following utterance which was recorded from a natural conversation:

> I can't imagine er if you got the city kind of plan of the city mapped out and I can't er quite map this bit on

It is ungrammatical in the sense that the speaker changes the structure of his speech several times. *Cannot* is elided to *can't* as is common in speech. It is impossible to judge whether (*you*) *got* is the past tense of *get*, which would not make particularly good sense but is not impossible, or whether it is an elided form of *have got* in which the auxiliary is completely inaudible. *Bit* is a lexical item much more frequently found in speech and *kind of* is used to make a noun (or verb or adjective) less precise, again in spoken language. Learners may not need to be taught to produce all these forms, but they do need to be taught to understand them.

The character of the *participants* in any speech event is also important. We may have a single producer and a single receiver of language. The receiver may be present and himself participating, or absent and doing no more than listen or read. There may be several participants, all actively engaged, or a single producer addressing an audience seen or unseen. Sometimes we produce language with no particular audience in mind at all. All of these and other situations will be reflected in the adjustments we make to our language. These adjustments are frequently quite automatic and we remain unaware of them, in our mother-tongue at least. Sometimes, however, we find ourselves quite consciously modifying our language, as when, for example, we are talking to a foreigner.

The participants in a speech event are important in another respect too. This is in the matter of the relationships between the individuals involved. Are the participants known to one another or are they strangers? Do they know each other well or only slightly? What is their relative social status and in what circumstances are they brought together in a particular speech event? It is largely factors of this kind that determine the relative formality of utterances, and the appropriate level is achieved by a combination of grammatical, lexical and phonological choices. The two sentences below contrast both grammatically and lexically:

> Candidates are requested to submit an application in triplicate
> Could you let us have three copies of your application?

The *physical context* of a speech event may also be relevant. Speaking on a telephone and writing a telegram impose conditions which will be reflected in the forms of language chosen. More importantly, the situational context in which language is being produced may give us a clue to another dimension, that of *domain*. Many uses of language take place in a characteristic setting. It may not be the setting as such that is important but the typical functions of the language that occur within that setting. Within an office we may hear or read language that is typically found in the domain of commerce; in a workshop much language will be typical of a technical or technological domain; in a school we will hear language in the domain of education. To some extent the language produced in these situations is predictable from our knowledge of the purposes for which it is produced, but in addition there are apparently arbitrary restrictions on the forms of language that are preferred or found acceptable in these situations.

Even if a learner had mastered the grammatical and stylistic features of language that we have discussed so far, he would still not know enough to ensure the correct construction and interpretation of utterances. We have not mentioned the speaker's purpose in making an utterance and the means whereby he can achieve the intended communicative effect. The same objective meaning can often be expressed in more than one way and the speaker's choice from these may depend, for example, on the particular element he wishes to emphasize or on how the information conveyed contrasts with what has already been said or is otherwise known to the speaker and hearer. In these cases the speaker's aim can be made fairly explicit by use of intonation or by reorganizing the structure of a sentence to focus attention on one part. There is, however, more to the speaker's purpose than this. Written and spoken utterances are produced with the intention of their having some effect on the person who will read or hear them, that is to say, they have some social function. That intention may simply be to report a piece of information, but it might equally be to advise, to enquire, to invite, to permit, to promise, to order, to direct, to deny, to express anger, surprise, pleasure, contempt or gratitude. Every native speaker has a knowledge of the way in which he can exploit the grammatical and lexical systems of his language to achieve these communicative functions. However, the potential that sentences of the grammar have for acting as utterances with particular communicative functions is not necessarily evident in the grammatical structure of the sentences themselves. Grammatically interrogative sentences are not used exclusively as questions. One can make comparisons without using comparatives. The point can be illustrated in a way that is very pertinent to language teaching.

The two sentences below might easily be brought together in language teaching materials because they have identical grammatical structure and might also be thought to be semantically analogous.

> Have you got a pencil?
> Have you got a house?

But if we consider them as potential utterances rather than as illustrations of certain grammatical facts of English, we will see that the speaker would be most unlikely to produce both these sentences with the same purpose. In a natural situation the most likely response to the former would be, 'Yes, here you are', whereas the answer to the latter could be, 'Yes, I bought one two years ago', or 'Yes, we live out at Wimbledon'. Often what is said is not meant and what is meant is not said. There is nothing devious about this. We have all learned to use our language in actual communication. It is as much a part of our language ability as is our command of grammar or our ability to pronounce it. In order to use and understand a language we need a *communicative* as well as a *grammatical* competence.

1.4 Vocabulary

We have discussed at some length a number of factors which enter systematically into the learner's interpretation of an utterance or the speaker's intention in expressing it. However, we have still not mentioned what most people will understand by *meaning*, that is, the meaning of words. The ability to refer to concrete and conceptual entities is as fundamental to language as is the capacity provided by the grammar to relate such entities to one another. Knowledge of a language demands mastery of its vocabulary as much as of its grammar.

The popular view of words is that they serve as labels for natural classes of objects and for 'concepts'. In learning another language, therefore, part of the task is that of attaching fresh labels to familiar things and ideas. This is as mistaken a notion about vocabulary as it is about syntax, since our classification of the physical and abstract world is itself determined by the lexical structure of the language we speak. If we learn a new language, we have to learn a new way of classifying things. Where languages are closely related to one another and where there are cultural similarities, there may be fairly close correspondences—though never complete identity—between parts of the lexical systems. Where languages are unrelated, the semantic differences will probably be quite marked. The lack of identity between words in different languages is easily demonstrated by the fact that two words are rarely translation equivalents in more than a small proportion of the types of linguistic context in which they occur.

The meaning of a lexical item is the product of the way in which it relates to other words and, at the same time, to non-linguistic reality. The relation to the non-linguistic world is evident in those words which can be used to refer to things, processes, qualities and so on. But it must not be forgotten that a good proportion of our vocabulary is an abstraction from this visible experience. Little of the vocabulary of this book can be associated directly with features of the physical world. More important, however, is the fact that even the concrete vocabulary cannot be regarded as the simple accumulation of isolated word meanings. Any one word is part of a larger, perhaps indeterminate set of words which relate to it in the degree to which they are substitutable for it, contrast with it or occur in similar linguistic contexts. Such relationships build up for each lexical item a network of associations which are as essential to the definition of the word's meaning as are the extra-linguistic associations. Just as the grammatical meaning of a linguistic form can be established only by reference to the grammatical system of which it is a part, so lexical meaning is the product of a word's place in the lexical system.

A simple example will make the point clear. Russian has one verb, *hoditj*, which means to go on foot and another, *jezditj*, which means to travel by vehicle, but no 'neutral' verb like 'go' which can be used for either. As teachers we could present learners with *hoditj* in a variety of appropriate physical contexts, but, particularly for example if the learners were native speakers of English, they would have no way of knowing that you cannot use this verb to refer to going somewhere by car. This fact, which is part of the meaning of *hoditj*, will only be established when they have further linguistic experience in the form of meeting the verb *jezditj*. Neither of these words can be properly understood without knowledge of the meaning of the other. These are not the only linguistic associations that are significant for these items. The pattern of relationships into which any word enters will be very intricate and will develop as long as we continue to use the language. Even in our mother-tongue we occasionally find something novel about the use of a word in its extralinguistic or linguistic context, and this will lead to some slight modification in its meaning even if it is only a matter of the connotations that the item will subsequently have for us.

The position for the learner is rather more complicated than this discussion of meaning has so far suggested. Each lexical form may have a number of different meanings, and how many meanings it has may well not be clear. There may be one form, *case*, but it has several clearly distinguished meanings or, as we might say, it constitutes a number of different *lexemes*. If we were told that someone knew the word *case*, we would want to know which lexeme it was that they knew. Was it *case* in the sense of suitcase, lawsuit, circumstance or as a grammatical term? These meanings are sufficiently distinct for us to say that what we have are four *homonyms*, four different lexical items that happen to have the same phonological and orthographical shape. But the problem lies in the fact that there is no clear boundary between examples such as these and those where we have what the native speaker will regard as simple extensions of a single lexeme, what is known as *polysemy*. To an English speaker it is self-evident that a *leg* is found not only on human beings, but on cuts of meat, on trousers and on chairs. To a Frenchman this is far from obvious. He can extend *jambe* to apply to trousers but not to meat (*gigot*) nor to a chair (*pied*). Polysemy is widespread in language, but the obvious problems that it can cause a learner may not be recognized by a teacher who does not speak the language of his pupils.

There is one further type of problem that faces the learner in his attempt to master the use of lexical items. Words which have compatible meanings do not always co-occur in a language. Since we can say *mother-tongue* and *native language* in English, why is it that *native tongue* is scarcely ever used and *mother language* is quite unacceptable? There is no answer to this question beyond saying that it is a characteristic of language that some combinations of words should be preferred to others. Some potential combinations may be semantically incompatible, of course, and the learner is unlikely to attempt to construct them. It should not be forgotten, though, that *idioms* are expressions whose meanings are not predictable from the meanings of their constituent parts. It can occasionally happen that, although the parts of an expression are incompatible, together they form a single, acceptable, idiomatic whole. There is no way in which the meaning of *in order to* can be worked out from a knowledge of the three words that make it up. The failure to use expected *collocations* and the occasional use of items that do not collocate are common indicators that a person who speaks a language fluently and with grammatical accuracy is not actually a native speaker. The learning of the potential collocability of lexical items probably takes place only through considerable exposure to the language.

1.5 Phonology

So far nothing has been said about the means by which language is actually expressed. We can use either the spoken or the written channel for communication. Most writing systems are based on a language's phonological system, and learning to write is largely a matter of mastering the orthographic conventions of the target language. We will not consider these further here. Speech is transmitted as a continuum of sound with occasional pauses, but it is perceived by the hearer as a succession of individual sounds. The individual sounds that a speaker combines into the continuum of speech are enormously varied. If we investigate speech instrumentally, we will discover that even the same word repeated by the same speaker will not be produced identically on the two occasions. Strictly speaking, the number of different sounds in any one person's pronunciation of a language might number hundreds or even thousands.

Fortunately some order can be brought to this diversity. Part of the variation is quite systematic and is seen to be conditioned by the position in the syllable in which a sound occurs or by the nature of the other sounds that are adjacent to it. In practice, therefore, even in our mother-tongue we are capable of perceiving something far less than the total, objective variety of sounds. We actually function in speech in terms of a system of significant sounds which is finite in any particular language. We can draw up an inventory of these sounds (phonemes), although a trained phonetician would be able to point out that each significant sound is realized in several different ways. The system therefore has an essentially abstract nature and in English, for example, contains 24 consonants and 20 vowels (including 8 diphthongs).

The learner's task in acquiring a second language is not so much to reach a native speaker's standard of pronunciation. It is not very realistic to expect this. He needs to acquire a pronunciation that is accurate enough for the significant sounds to be distinctive from one another. There is not necessarily a single pronunciation of the sound that will enable him to do this. In the case of English /p/ and /b/ the distinction between the two phonemes is marked by aspiration in *pall* and *ball*, by the voicing of the following consonant in *plight* and *blight* and by the length of the preceding vowel in *mop* and *mob*.

The important thing in pronunciation is not whether a sound can be produced adequately in isolation, but how well it is formed in the phonological contexts in which it occurs in the target language. A sound may not be intrinsically difficult for a learner, but if it occurs in an unfamiliar context, he may find it as hard to produce correctly as he would if it were a totally novel sound to him. The particular combinations of sounds that are found in a language may also cause problems. Initial and final consonant clusters can be especially difficult for learners whose own languages do not possess them.

It must not be forgotten either that there is more to pronunciation than the ability to pronounce isolated words accurately. Words do not often occur naturally in isolation. They are embedded in the stream of speech. The phonetics of connected speech is not the same as that of individual words. In order to be intelligible in

C

speech the learner has to master the phonetic characteristics of connected speech. In natural speech sounds are elided and assimilated. That is to say sounds and syllables may disappear completely or their pronunciation may undergo considerable modification under the influence of neighbouring sounds. For example, *and* in English is scarcely ever pronounced /ænd/. According to the context in which it occurs, it may be realized as /ən/, /n/, /əm/ or /m/. There will be characteristic rhythmic patterns which, as in the case of English, may have the further effect of changing the quality of vowels. The imposition of incorrect rhythmic patterns on a language can interfere more with effective communication than can the faulty production of an individual sound.

Most important of all is intonation. Languages have characteristic ways of using the pitch of the voice. It follows recognized contours of movement, focusing by means of stress or change of direction on particular parts of the utterance. Although it is difficult to assign meaning to a particular contour in the abstract, the correct interpretation of any spoken utterance would be quite impossible without taking intonation into account. The functions of intonation are not necessarily the same in all languages, and certainly the actual forms and meanings of intonation patterns differ. In English, intonation may have an affective function. We can express emotions like surprise, irony, sympathy, doubt or contempt. But it can also express grammatical meaning.

I only touched the glass

By intonation we can indicate whether *only* is associated with *touched* or with *glass*. We can also change the function of a sentence, turning a declarative sentence into a question or an interrogative into an exclamation. Because of the redundancy of language an error in the pronunciation of an individual sound rarely affects communication, whereas an error in intonation can lead to a different interpretation being put on an utterance. For this reason the acquisition of an accurate intonation may be a higher priority than the learning of individual sounds.

2 Language acquisition and language learning

2.1 Introduction

In the preceding chapter we have seen what the perfect native speaker's knowledge of his language consists of. It is very rare for an individual to develop as comprehensive a knowledge of a foreign language as the native speaker. However, the process of learning a foreign language is essentially the growing control of the different components of language that have been described above. To state what the various elements of language knowledge are, however, is to say nothing about how they might best be learned. To take a very obvious but none the less fundamental point, does the fact that we can isolate the different aspects of language for the purpose of analysis and description mean that, in teaching, the components of language should initially be taught separately and then subsequently re-synthesized? Or can effective learning take place when whole samples of language in use are being presented to the learner? However good our understanding of the nature of language, it cannot help us to answer a question of this sort. Nor can it tell us what factors promote language learning and what factors hinder it. In order to establish what principles should be followed in the teaching of foreign languages, we therefore have to look not only at the nature of language itself but also at what is known about the nature of language learning.

Actually there is very little that is known incontrovertibly about language learning, although there are many strongly-held beliefs. It might be enlightening to begin by considering some aspects of the way in which a child learns his or her mother tongue, not because we wish to assume that language teaching should imitate as closely as possible the 'natural' process of language acquisition but because it will enable us to see some of the conditions under which language acquisition *can* take place and we might find this helps us to understand the process of language learning.*

2.2 Language acquisition

If we consider the child's acquisition of language between the ages of about twelve months and five years, a first thing we might observe is that the quantity of language involved is enormous. The child may well be in contact with language for most of his waking hours. This contact will take different forms. Some of it will be language directed at the child by other people, particularly parents. A strong effort will be made to ensure that this language is meaningful to the child. This may be done by demonstrating relevant objects and actions in the surroundings, by an intuitive attempt at simplification of the language, or, in later stages, by actual explanations.

There will be other language that the child is exposed to, in the sense that it is produced in his presence, but which will not be addressed to him and most of which will not be meaningful to him, at least in the early stages of his language acquisition.

Finally there will be language that the child himself produces. Part of this will be addressed to other people, but it would be a mistake to think that such language represents all or even most of the child's language production. At a certain stage in his language development he is likely to spend many hours in monologue and imaginative dialogue, regardless of whether there is anyone else present to stimulate him.

There are some other significant factors about the language that the child is exposed to. In the first place it is, of course, spoken language. Secondly, what the child hears is also linguistically-uncontrolled language. By this is meant that there is nothing like the

* The term *language acquisition* is used here for the process where a language is acquired as a result of natural and largely random exposure to language, the term *language learning* where the exposure is structured through language teaching.

isolation and repetition of a single sentence structure that is a characteristic of much language teaching. The child acquires his language without having it predigested for him in this way. It has already been noted that adults do often make the attempt to simplify their language for the benefit of the child, but what they produce remains structurally varied and, it is sometimes suggested, even makes things more complicated for the child. One observation that has been made is that the child may play language games with himself which involve repeating the same type of sentence perhaps with minimal alterations, and that this does resemble some productive exercises in language teaching.

The language in the child's environment is also uncontrolled in the sense that it is not made up of perfect samples of grammatical speech. Like all natural speech it is subject to many distortions, omissions and inconsistencies. It is never a direct reflection of the somewhat idealized form of language that is described in Grammars. In spite of this the child has the capacity to learn from it and to learn to understand it.

A somewhat self-evident point is that the child learns whatever language he is exposed to. Most children are in contact with one language only and, of course, they become monolinguals. It should not be forgotten, however, that where children are brought up in a consistently bilingual environment, they acquire both languages simultaneously, though with some retardation when compared with monolingual children. There is an initial merging of the two languages, but subsequently they are separated and remain functionally quite distinct.

More interesting perhaps than the language to which the child is exposed is his reaction to it. We have already seen that when he is adequately exposed to language he will produce language himself. In part, what he produces is an imitation of what he has heard and this is a process which adults often try to stimulate, but, contrary to what has generally been thought, a good deal of his language production is not imitative at all. Not only does he have the ability to take words and phrases that he has heard and use them in new combinations, he also actually produces pieces of language that he could not have heard from the other people in his environment.

An utterance of the following kind would be entirely typical of children's language:

> Daddy better go work, bettern't he

The 'incorrectness' of the first part of the sentence seems to be simply a matter of faulty imitation, but no model sample of language has ever been presented to the child that could have led him to produce *better* in the tag by a process of imitation.

The child has an ability to generalize his knowledge of language beyond what he has actually experienced. Quite unconsciously he is discovering that there is a grammatical system at work in the stream of sound to which he is constantly exposed. He makes the assumption that pieces of language that behave similarly in one context are likely to behave similarly in another. It is on this basis that his own language is produced. It only becomes noticeable when a mistake is made. The child is unaware of the *had* that usually precedes *better* and therefore associates *better* with words like *can* and *must* which he has heard preceding *go*. Since *can* and *must* occur in tags, it should also be possible to use *better*. In this instance the child has constructed his utterance according to grammatical rules which are not the rules of adult language. With wider experience of the language his utterances will approximate more and more closely to the utterances that an adult might produce.

Whether the child is able to do this, as some linguists and psychologists have claimed, because human beings have a specific and innate language learning ability, or whether it is merely a specific instance of some more general learning capacity that is applied to other kinds of human learning too, does not matter greatly when it comes to the teaching of languages. The significant thing is that what is learned is more than what is experienced and that this learning is creative in the sense that the learner can express what he has not heard.

What the child discovers when he makes a mistake is that there is some kind of limit to the way in which the rules of language operate, of which, in a practical sense, he has been unaware. He discovers the limitation, that is to say, provided he knows that he has made a mistake. To know this, there must be some process of feedback in operation. In language acquisition there are various ways in which this feedback is provided. The adults present might make a more or less formal correction, not, of course, with the use of grammatical terminology, but simply by telling the child that he has made a mistake and should have said something different. More likely is that the adults themselves will be unaware that they are providing any feedback at all. It has been observed that parents sometimes repeat in a fully grammatical form a less than grammatical utterance produced by a child.

To an utterance like

Mummy go shop

the mother might respond

Yes, that's right. Mummy's going to the shops.

In this way the child's reduced utterance and the parent's fully grammatical utterance are brought into immediate juxtaposition.

The success of a child's attempt at communication may be apparent to him in various ways. Other people present may show obvious signs of approval or disapproval; they may react verbally themselves, thereby showing that the child has conveyed whatever he intended to convey; the stimulus to the child's utterance may have been the desire to have a particular need met, say, the need for a drink or for a toy. If, in response to the child's utterance, the drink or the toy is provided, he knows that the form of his utterance has proved acceptable, at least at that stage of language development.

It also seems likely that the child can provide his own feedback, in that he may modify the rules according to which he is constructing his utterances even where no direct feedback has been provided. It must be supposed that even on the basis simply of hearing language correctly used by others, the child can refine the system he is using. Sometimes errors in a child's language persist in spite of correction, but then they disappear, almost—as it seems—when the child is ready to master the particular linguistic generalization involved. Since there do seem to be broad developmental stages in language acquisition, this notion may not be as fanciful as it appears.

The feedback that is provided by other people does more than simply inform the child whether or not his message is correctly formed. It also demonstrates to him that his language has an effect on the behaviour of others. Rather than being at the mercy of the environment, to some extent, through language, he can bring the environment under his own control. It would be fairly meaningless to say that this motivates him to learn the language. What it does mean is that he is becoming aware of the regulatory function of language. Through language, he learns, his needs can be met. At first the needs will be material, but later they may include the need for information, advice, permission and so on.

As long as adequate exposure to language is provided, the process of language acquisition that has just been described will be followed by all children who do not suffer some physiological or psychological defect. The rates of learning will not be identical, but they will not be wildly different either. By the age of five a substantial proportion of the grammatical system of the language will have been mastered by all children. Given that children may have very different intellectual endowments, it is the similarities not the dissimilarities in their linguistic development that are so striking.

2.3 Language learning

We cannot depend wholly on this understanding of language acquisition when we turn our attention to language learning. As we shall see, the conditions of learning are not identical in the two cases. We should also keep in mind evidence that is available from psychological research, and given that a great deal of uncertainty remains, we should not ignore more subjectively-held views.

One question that has to be discussed before all others is whether languages are *learned* by the same psychological processes as they are *acquired*. The discussion of language acquisition has centred entirely on children, but adults too may find themselves in a language-acquisition situation, although inevitably the situation will be bilingual not monolingual. When adults and children experience what is apparently the same bilingual situation, it is commonly observed that the children learn more effectively. But the *apparently* here may be important. Although they may be surrounded by people using the second language they are rarely wholly cut off from the use of the mother-tongue, and the social pressures on them to learn the new language are rarely as intense as are the pressures on children once they start school. So the lesser achievement may be due not so much to the loss of the ability to induce the facts of the language system from exposure as to fundamentally less favourable conditions of learning. At worst, there may be a slow atrophy of the inductive capacity with age, but it is very doubtful whether it is lost altogether.

The most obvious difference between younger and older learners in actual language performance will occur in the relative masteries of the pronunciation system. Many adults who otherwise acquire an excellent command of language never overcome the difficulties posed by a new sound system. For this there are possible neurological explanations. On the other hand, the older learner can call upon learning abilities which have not yet been developed in small children. They can recognize the overall objectives of language learning. They can identify and make explicit the aim of any particular learning sequence. They can bring to bear deductive and analytical abilities. They can sustain mental effort and perhaps motivation over longer periods. These are capacities that have been developed in the general process of education. Older learners are therefore able to exploit a wider range of learning strategies than younger children, so that their actual achievement can be well ahead of that of children. It would accord with our subjective impressions of language learners if we asserted that individuals differ in the strategies of learning that they prefer to adopt or from which they most easily learn. This would be in contrast with the acquisition of language where the same processes are involved for everybody.

The most obvious contrast between the language-learning and the language-acquisition situations is in the amount of exposure to language. Intensive courses apart, language teaching provides for from two to six hours a week during up to forty weeks of the year. One year in the classroom provides the equivalent of from one to three weeks' contact in a language-acquisition situation. If it takes from three to four years for a child to learn his mother-tongue to a reasonable degree of proficiency, we can work out for ourselves the astronomical length of time it would take for language learning to reach the same level if it was based on the same kind of largely random exposure to language.

It follows that ways must be found of facilitating the learner's process of inducing the grammatical system from the language data to which he is exposed. One way is to restrict or organize his exposure to the language so that he is not presented with linguistically diverse forms, but with samples of language that exemplify some linguistically significant generalization. This strategy is followed in the construction of most language-teaching materials. A new learning unit will contain an unfamiliar linguistic form which occurs in many examples and which the learner is given maximal opportunities to produce. It is plausible that the linguistic rule represented in the actual sentences experienced will be more rapidly learned in this way than if no linguistic considerations influenced the choice of language that was to be presented to the learner. A succession of linguistically-structured units might well be more effective overall than a similar quantity of random material.

The other way of short-cutting the inductive processes is to exploit analytical abilities, especially those of older learners. This means formulating quite explicitly the linguistic generalizations that underlie the construction of learning units such as the one referred to above. Small children probably do not yet possess the ability either to comprehend or to make explicit statements about linguistic structures. It is hardly surprising, therefore, if such statements are absent from natural language acquisition. But adults do possess such abilities, and although the verbalization of language rules is not the aim of language learning, it seems perverse to ignore the possible benefits of making explicit just *what* is being learned. In any case many older learners will expect linguistic rules to be made explicit to them, and learning can be hindered where expectations are not fulfilled.

Making the linguistic generalizations explicit will not be detrimental to language learning provided it does not become the dominant language activity. This latter danger is one case of a principle which is well illustrated in language acquisition and which is one of the few highly reliable principles of language learning. On the whole, what people learn is determined by or reflected in the nature of the activities they engage in. One aspect of the child's exposure to language is that he spends much more time hearing or listening to language than he does producing it. This is directly reflected in the type of language ability that he develops. The child from a very early age understands a far wider range of linguistic forms than he produces himself. Indeed, this is not only characteristic of the child still engaged on the task of acquiring a language, it is characteristic of the mature speaker too. We are all capable of understanding far more language than we actually produce ourselves. We actually spend far more time receiving language than producing it, so the difference is hardly surprising.

But important and neglected as the true relationship between production and reception is, it is the underlying principle that is to be emphasized here. If we look at the language-learning activity overall, the language achievement will reflect fairly accurately the components of that activity. We can judge the value of the language-learning activity against the true and full nature of language as outlined in the first chapter. If the language-learning activity is substantially the reciting of paradigms, the achievement will be largely the ability to recite paradigms. If time is spent doing dictations, it will be the ability to convert spoken language into written symbols that will be learned. If the preoccupation of a course is with mechanical, spoken drills, it will not be spoken *language* that is learned, since this involves more than a mastery of the formal elements of the grammatical code.

This is not to say that none of these activities can contribute to language learning. In knowing a language we need to master paradigmatic relations. We should be able to associate speech and writing. We must have control of the forms of language in order to express its meanings. In any case some transfer between skills will take place. But the totality of language-learning activity should reflect all those components of language knowledge that are necessary to meet the objectives of learning.

This is one reason why repetition has long been thought an important principle in language teaching. What is ensured by repeti-

tion of linguistic forms—whether *by* the learner or *to* the learner—
is a frequency of contact which should be reflected in the subse-
quent knowledge that the learner has of the language. Without wishing to assert that the number of repetitions determines exactly the strength of the learning, nor to deny that a form
that has been encountered only once can on occasions be learned,
the fact that a form has been used on a number of occasions increases
the likelihood that the learner will be able to use it and will use
it in the future. Just as repeated opportunity to speak the language
will tend to lead to a greater capacity for speaking the language, so
too requiring the learner repeatedly to distinguish between past and
perfect tenses makes it more likely that they will be accurately
distinguished subsequently.

It is important, however, to bear in mind that what is being
learned in this way depends upon the nature of the activity. No
matter how many opportunities the learner has to identify and
produce the formal distinction between past and perfect, he will
not thereby learn the semantic distinction. The contribution of
any repeated language activity still has to be measured against what
we know to be the total nature of language.

If, because of the relative paucity of the exposure to language,
the decision is taken to introduce some kind of linguistic structuring,
it is very likely that this will result in some lessening in the diversity
of the linguistic structure to which the learner is exposed. This
then creates a situation for the language learner that is unlike that
faced by the small child. We saw that it is a characteristic of language
acquisition that there is a great range of linguistic structure in the
child's experience and that this structure does not occur in the
pure and idealized form that is described in Grammars but is subject
to all the normal distortions of everyday language. It is impossible
to know whether this heterogeneity is necessary for the learning
process, but one result is that the child does develop the capacity
to understand everyday speech in spite of the difficulties that it
apparently presents. Following the principle that has just been
elucidated, if the learner's exposure to language is only exposure to
carefully-controlled language, it is only this kind of language that
he will learn to comprehend. The fact that language learners do

often in practice find inordinate difficulty in transferring their ability to understand classroom language into an ability to understand language spoken naturally outside the classroom provides some confirmation of the principle itself. At the same time it suggests that there are dangers in rigid linguistic control, and that adequate opportunity needs to be provided for the learner to meet the language in all its diversity. By diversity is meant language that is rich in its structural range and realistic in its actualization. Such language might well not have been produced specifically for the language learner at all.

The language learner is expected to respond productively to his exposure to language just as the child does. As with the child learning his mother-tongue, the responses may be imitative, but it is similarly the case that such imitative responses are not enough to ensure language learning. Imitation ensures that the sentences uttered are correctly formed, but it fails to meet several other conditions that are necessary for language learning. Using a language is as much a matter of making choices from the grammatical system as of knowing by which forms those choices are realized once they have been made. As long as production is in the form of imitation, nothing is being learned about how the choices of language form are made. For this the learner himself needs to be put in the position of having to make choices. Even this can be done in a relatively controlled fashion, as when the learner is given the opportunity to choose between two tenses or between two cases following a given preposition. But this still has a considerable element of imitation and falls well short of the freedom that an ordinary speaker of language has to exercise. The same applies to the modern drilling technique of the analogical production of sentences. Given a model sentence the learner is expected to produce further sentences of like structure, perhaps with marginal changes, perhaps using given words and phrases. Here too choice is almost wholly absent and we have, in effect, disguised imitation. For language learning to be entirely effective the learner must be provided with opportunities to choose freely not only from among the forms that are the immediate subject of the teaching but from all the forms of language that have been learned up to that point. Without such opportunities the learner will never master the creative use of language and this, as we have seen, is how his achievement is ultimately to be judged.

There is another reason, linguistic rather than psychological, why controlled language use does not ensure learning. As has been noted, imitation ensures that correct forms are produced, but it does not tell the learner anything about the boundaries of correctness. If he is expected only to experience those occasions where a particular form is correctly used, he cannot know what would be the occasions when it would be incorrect to use it. No matter how many words like *narrow*, *shallow* and *likely* are presented to the learner in the comparative forms *narrower*, *shallower*, *likelier*, and no matter how many times he repeats these and other correct forms, he will not know that many other disyllabic adjectives, such as *useful*, *solid*, and *childish* cannot form their comparatives morphologically. No-one is likely to use controlled language teaching deliberately to induce such incorrect forms. It follows that the only way that the learner will discover that such forms are not possible is when he makes mistakes with them in his free use of language. For this reason too, therefore, it is essential that adequate opportunity for free use of language be provided as part of the language-learning process.

This further implies that mistakes are an inevitable and indeed necessary part of the process of learning a language. But mistakes will only be useful to the learner if he gets the feedback that enables him to learn from his mistakes. The situation is strictly analogous to the language-acquisition situation. Where the learner has not yet fully learned a form in the second language or where, as we have seen, he is unsure of the domain of the rules he is acquiring, he will tend to make mistakes. These mistakes will be systematically of two types. He may overgeneralize the second language form, so that in the example given above he might produce the form *usefuller*. Alternatively he may fall back upon the linguistic forms he already knows—those of the mother-tongue. In this case his lack of knowledge will be shown in the form of interference from the first language. The first type of mistake is highly characteristic of monolingual language acquisition too. The second, of course, cannot occur in that situation.

The feedback will be provided principally by the teacher—his acceptance or approval if an utterance is correctly formed, a formal correction if a mistake has occurred, the latter being more effective if it is given immediately the mistake has been made. The learner's own capacity to identify feedback is exploited in the language-laboratory situation where his own production is immediately followed by the correct form, on the assumption that any error can thereby be corrected by the learner himself. Research suggests that this feedback does not always operate efficiently and that the learner needs to be trained to recognize it. Feedback will also be provided through the learner's wider exposure to language, since his own performance will be modified as a result of his reading and listening.

Given that mistakes are a normal part of the process of learning, there is no reason why they should be strongly deprecated nor why strenuous efforts should be made to avoid the possibility of learners making mistakes. This is as well, since the learner's desire to avoid at all costs actually committing an error in the second language and his fear of correction by the teacher have a markedly inhibiting effect on his attempts to use the language at all freely. There is consequently a considerable degree of conflict between the requirement that correction should take place when an error has been made, so that the necessary feedback is provided, and the desirability of the learner's regarding his errors as relatively insignificant when measured against the value of his attempting to use the language freely and communicatively. Obviously the teacher must be sensitive in his use of correction.

One striking contrast between the language-learning and the language-acquisition situations is that whereas, in language acquisition, language learning and language use are one and the same activity, in language learning the two are very largely distinct. The child learning the mother-tongue either addresses his language to other children or adults or else engages in imaginative language activity. This activity may take the form of a monologue, often with an imagined interlocutor, or a dialogue in which the child performs both the roles in a conversation. For the child, at this stage of linguistic development, even in the absence of an addressee, these are none the less acts of communication. The imagined and the real world are not readily distinguished from one another. By the time children are of an age to be taught a foreign language a division between the two has taken place. They will no longer take an imagined situation for a real one.

It was suggested above that the need to communicate and the recognition of the regulatory function of language would provide a very powerful motivation for learning a second language. In language acquisition adults tend to learn a second language to the level that is necessary for them to meet whatever communication needs they can themselves identify. It is a form of motivation that ought to be exploited more fully in language learning. Unfortunately it presents various problems. In existing teaching practice very little of what takes place in the classroom is communicative use of language at all. Most activity is preparing learners for language use, not actually engaging them in it. It is supposed that when the system has been mastered, the learners will be able to use it. Because of the division between the imaginative and the real that has taken place, even those activities which resemble true communicative behaviour are not really such. Role-playing and the use of dialogues are replicas of communication, not communication itself, since the urge to communicate has not arisen from the participants themselves but has been stimulated from outside by the teacher. It remains desirable, however, that ways should be found of bridging the gap between the artificiality of the language class and the truly communicative use of the language. If the desire to communicate through the language can be created in learners, there is little that could be more motivating and could do more to ensure effective learning.

As it is, with this form of motivation rarely operating in language learning, research has tended to contrast two essentially different types of motivation. On the one hand there are learners who are interested in the language and culture for its own sake and who are potentially sympathetic to the values of a different society; and on the other hand there are learners who are learning a language for some specific purpose, perhaps because it is going to be useful to them in some way. Of these two types it tends to be the former who are the more successful language learners and it is presumably a learner of this type that we commonly describe as being 'well-motivated'. Not surprisingly, success in learning a language may itself be instrumental in developing good motivation.

One of the factors which promotes language learning is the relative meaningfulness of the language being learned. From the linguistic point of view it is essential that the learner should know the meaning of the linguistic forms he is learning. Obviously the semantic system of a language cannot be learned through types of language practice where meaning is absent. This is self-evident where word meaning is concerned, but it applies equally to grammatical meaning. A learner may be required to repeat and manipulate sentences in which he understands every individual lexical item, but he cannot possibly understand the structural relations between those items—one aspect of grammatical meaning—unless the meaning of the sentence as a whole is known to him. From the linguistic point of view, therefore, learning will be incomplete if the contact with the second language is not meaningful.

More than this, however, research suggests that learning proceeds more rapidly and what is learned is better retained when the language involved is fully meaningful. There are two aspects to this meaningfulness. First, the wider the range of associations that is built up for the linguistic forms the better. We saw in the first chapter that this is linguistically necessary for the acquisition of meaning, but here the point is more a psychological one. The wider and richer the network of associations that any form possesses for the learner, the less the likelihood of that form being forgotten. Secondly, the learning of sentences that are semantically and structurally well formed, sentences whose meaning and grammatical structure are easily acceptable to the learner, is easier and more permanent than the learning of sentences that are deviant in any way. Even the formal aspects of language themselves are more readily acquired when they occur in a meaningful context. This suggests that types of learning that are devoted exclusively to the learning of formal elements are actually less efficient even in meeting their more limited objectives than those that require the language to be meaningful throughout the learning process. For these reasons language learning should take place in a rich linguistic and cultural

D

environment, where the learner is conscious of the semantic potential of the forms he meets and produces as actual, acceptable utterances in the language.

Where methodologists wish to argue from the language-acquisition analogy, they commonly refer to the fact that the language learned is exclusively spoken language, and tend to argue accordingly that language teaching should focus on spoken language. A discussion of the exact place of spoken and written language in language teaching can be left to the last chapter. Here we can limit ourselves to one or two observations about the learning of language.

It is true that for five years or more virtually all children experience language only in its spoken form. On the other hand, for ontogenetic reasons this is inevitable. At that age children do not have the capacities to make the somewhat abstract connection between spoken and written language. Nor do they have the necessary motor and perceptive skills. There is therefore no alternative. If we were to consider adults in a language-acquisition situation, we would be far less sure that they could not benefit from contact with the written form of language. No doubt they would have great difficulty in learning from the written form alone, but this is not really the point. The question is whether it is psychologically necessary or advantageous for speech to be learned before writing. Where laboratory research has been done into learning in the two modalities, speech and writing, it has usually demonstrated that, with adults at least, simultaneous presentation of language in both modalities facilitates language learning. To put it in simple terms, people learn what they see *and* hear more readily than something which they only hear. Since almost all language learners are of an age where the written channel is open to them, arguments about the place of speech based on the analogy of child language acquisition are not very strong.

There are a number of other psychological factors which have no parallel in language acquisition. For example, it is a common belief among learners and teachers alike that some people have an aptitude for languages. Whether such aptitude is innate or the product of previous learning experience is not really relevant. If there is such a thing as language aptitude, it means that individuals bring with them different language-learning potentials and that their language-learning performance can be expected to reflect this. If this potential involves something other than a general intelligence factor, we can designate it as a specifically *language* aptitude. In any real teaching situation it may seem to be the only possible explanation of the very different achievements of different individuals. However, such research as has been done has not really succeeded in isolating a specifically linguistic component in language aptitude, although there is a suggestion that it relates to phonetic rather than any other linguistic skills.

A point derived from research into learning in general rather than into language learning itself relates to the degree to which a learning task requires all of the learner's attention. In language teaching it is easy to distinguish between learning tasks which can be easily completed with only a part of the learner's attention engaged, and those which can be successfully completed only if the learner gives the whole of his attention to it. Since the engagement of the whole of the learner's attention presumably also means the engagement of his whole learning potential, there will be advantage in devising learning tasks which demand full application of the learner's faculties. Tasks which require only a proportion of the learner's attention will be less efficient in exploiting his learning potential and in any case will permit some of his attention to be directed to things other than the learning task in hand.

We saw in the first chapter that knowing a language cannot be a matter of the memorization of sentences, since this does not account for the creativity of language. However, we should not deduce from this that memory is not an important factor in language learning. Already in the earlier discussion learning has been glossed in terms of ease of acquisition and of retention. Obviously there is little benefit in learning something initially if it is not then retained. We have seen that factors like the meaningfulness of linguistic forms and the number of associations made to them affect retention. Here it is necessary only to add that continued contact with a form also ensures its retention. If a form is learned, no matter how many times it was repeated by the learner at the time of learning, it will be less and less likely to be recalled correctly as time passes without any further contact with it. The implication is obviously that we should ensure the recurrence of forms once they have been taught. If we do not, the initial learning is likely to have to be undertaken all over again.

Mention should also be made of short-term memory. The ability to repeat a linguistic structure or a number of linguistic structures immediately upon the hearing of that structure is more or less dependent upon one's proficiency in the language. The greater the proficiency, the longer and the more complex the forms that can be repeated accurately within a short time-span. More significant is the converse, that level of language proficiency places limitations on short-term memory. There is no point in engaging the learner in language activities which require him to store more language in his short-term memory than his level of proficiency permits. This can easily happen in the use of purely oral language drills, and the result can be that mistakes are actually induced by the form of the drill rather than by the intrinsic difficulty for the learner of the forms he is being expected to produce.

3 Environmental factors in learning

3.1 Introduction

We have now looked at the subject-matter of language learning and we have seen those characteristics of learners which will tend to promote or hinder learning and which teaching can be planned to cater for. However, we have not yet accounted for all the factors that determine learning. The teacher will be faced with many other factors, largely beyond his own control but none the less important in deciding whether or not his pupils learn the foreign language. In general these will be features of the narrower and the broader contexts in which learning and teaching are to take place and they are grouped together here under the heading of *environmental factors*. For all that linguistic and psychological factors have very general significance for our understanding of language learning, the teacher faced with decisions on the methods and techniques that he is to adopt has to bear in mind the conditions under which he will be working. In other words, we cannot say that particular methods are good or bad regardless of the circumstances in which they are being used. It would be a bad teacher who did not take into account his own qualities as a teacher, the characteristics of his pupils and the physical and other conditions in which he had to work.

3.2 The educational context

One important feature of the learning context is that of *time*. In the designing of a language course or syllabus the question of how many hours are available for teaching will obviously do much to determine what level of attainment can be reached. At one extreme there may be no more than fifty or sixty hours of instruction; at the other there could be as many as a thousand. If the number of contact hours is beyond the teacher's control, he must set his objectives to what can reasonably be achieved in the time available. If it is the objectives that are predetermined and the time dimension that is variable, the teacher will have to judge the amount of time that he will need to meet the objectives that have been set. It can happen that the teacher finds himself in a situation in which he does not have control of either dimension. The objectives have been set for him and he has only a fixed, and often inadequate, amount of time to reach the objectives. Alternatively he may have to prepare his pupils for a final examination which does not reflect the objectives for which he would like to prepare his pupils or, indeed, which often does not embody any clear understanding of learning objectives at all. Apart from agitating for reform of a system which imposes unrealistic requirements on both teacher and learner, the teacher can only effect some kind of compromise between what he is expected to achieve, what he would like to achieve and what conditions permit him to achieve. This is not the place to spell out how such compromises might be made. It might involve being realistic enough to recognize which objectives can be met and which cannot. Some aspects of the learners' language knowledge might be brought to the point of practical effectiveness, others might be left latent. Since the future of the pupils usually depends upon success in examinations, the teacher cannot ignore them, no matter how much he may disapprove of them, but perhaps he can employ methods that ensure that learning for the examination is not the only kind of learning that takes place. Any decisions that the teacher himself takes along these lines will have methodological implications.

However, *intensity* is no less important an aspect of time than quantity. The frequency of the learner's contact with the second language is possibly a more significant variable than the total amount. In conventional school language learning, the contact can be as little as two hours a week. It is rarely more than five or six hours a week. Intensive courses, on the other hand, often provide from fifteen to twenty hours a week of instruction, while also requiring work to be done outside the classroom which significantly increases the quantity of exposure. It is impossible to suggest strict numerical limits at either end, but the dangers of too little or too much are probably similar. In both cases there may be boredom and loss of motivation. If the contact is as little as two hours a week, it will be difficult to inculcate a sense of progress and achievement and there will be serious lack of interest in learning. If there is contact for more than twenty hours a week, there may be fatigue. Almost certainly more intensive exposure than is normally provided is desirable. With only two hours a week available, learning by the normal inductive processes is probably very difficult. What is more, there is a serious danger of forgetting when the contact is so sparse. When the intensity is inadequate, the quantity will have to be increased or the objectives will have to be reduced. Where short-duration, intensive courses are provided, the learning achievement will be much more evident and there will be greater productivity for the overall investment of time. On the other hand an observation that is sometimes made, but which has not been sufficiently investigated, is that what is quickly learned is quickly forgotten. No doubt any danger here would be overcome provided some contact with the language were maintained after teaching had been completed.

A much more commonly discussed variable than time is the number of pupils in the class. Once again it is neither possible nor even particularly necessary to suggest that there is an optimal size for a class of language learners. No doubt eighty is too many and one is too few, but the real problems arise with classes that are too large rather than with those that are too small. The question to be considered is whether 'desirable' methods and objectives can be maintained in the face of classes of more than, say, forty pupils. The solution that is usually offered is not to treat the class as a single learning unit, but to split it up into smaller groups, so that both teaching methods and objectives need undergo little or no modification. For this to be successful much will depend on the qualities of the individual teacher and on the conditions in which he or she is working. Where these circumstances are the most favourable, a fair degree of success can be achieved in reaching the most difficult of objectives—oral proficiency in the language—and in using the most demanding of methods—an oral method. It is more realistic to admit that in many cases neither these objectives nor these methods are suitable. It is far easier to engage the attention of even a very large class of learners on the learning task when the objectives focus more on written than on spoken language. A very real and valuable language achievement is possible. If the class has to be treated as a single teaching unit, more explicitly analytical approaches may well prove more successful than inductive techniques. In a large class it is very difficult to arrange for every individual to have the intensive contact with the language (especially spoken language) that is necessary for his inductive processes to operate effectively. Decisions about methods to be adopted cannot be taken without regard for the number of pupils in the class and the conditions in which they are learning.

The physical arrangements too cannot be ignored. Classes cannot be split into groups if classroom furnishings are immovable fixtures, if the groups would have to be placed so close that they would interfere with one another, if they are not allowed or are not able to leave the classroom itself. Where desks are placed very closely together, where classrooms are overcrowded, methods of language teaching that require movement and activity from the pupils produce such physical disturbances and difficulties that concentration is hard to sustain and the pace of teaching can become so slow as to be ineffective. If different classes are being taught in one large room, the use of choral techniques may be too much of a disturbance to other classes. The inadequacy of lighting can make reading a very difficult process, especially if the pupils are rather a long way from the blackboard. There is no point in attempting to list exhaustively all the physical impediments that can occur in the context of learning. They are usually apparent enough. The important thing is that in devising his overall strategy for teaching, the teacher should not ignore the situation in which his teaching has to be done. There is no virtue in setting objectives which are unrealistic in the conditions of learning in which the teacher actually has to work.

The final element in the physical context of learning is the stock of resources which the teacher will be able to exploit. A language-teaching situation may be characterized by the presence or absence of all or any of the following: textbooks, supplementary readers, workbooks, exercise-books, writing-paper, drawing-paper, pens, pencils, chalk, blackboard, tapes, tape-recorders, language laboratories, wall-pictures, wall-charts, flannel-boards, other display facilities, slides, filmstrips, ciné-films, television, radio, record-players, video-recorders, closed-circuit television and libraries. Naturally enough, what can be achieved in any situation will depend on the resources that are available. Conversely the absence of certain resources will place serious limitations on what the teacher can achieve. You cannot teach people to read if adequate reading material is not available. They cannot learn to understand natural spoken language if no means exists for them to hear natural spoken language. An awareness of what resources are available is necessary from the beginning of a teaching operation. It should not be the case that the teacher first decides his objectives, then determines his methods and only finally comes to the question of what resources are available and how he will exploit them. The objectives themselves should be defined with an awareness of what the resources will permit or, if the teacher is very favourably placed, of what resources he will need to obtain in order to reach the objectives in the most efficient way. Resources are not an adjunct, but an integral part of the learning situation. Their availability offers opportunities to the teacher. The lack of them imposes restrictions which may mean that his pupils cannot be set the objectives that he would like them to reach and cannot be taught by the methods that would otherwise be the most suitable.

3.3 The social context

As well as these features of the actual learning situation itself, there are factors in the wider social context that influence language learning. Particularly important in the case of language learning are certain attitudes which are characteristic of the society to which the learner belongs. Some cultures expect a reasonably high degree of bilingualism to be a normal quality of the educated man or woman. Typically, though not exclusively, they will be societies whose own language is not widely spoken. In terms of natural language acquisition they might be monolingual societies. We are not concerned here with communities where bilingualism develops as a result of frequent language contact with more than one language. In spite of the fact that there may be no great pressure to learn the foreign language for use within the learner's own community, the level of proficiency reached is surprisingly high. Explanations for this in terms of the better qualifications of teachers or the greater efficiency of the methods they use do not stand up to close examination, since the same results are not obtained in other societies where language teaching is carried out in much the same way. Nor is there any evidence that some peoples have a gift for languages. When a comparison is made between language-learning achievement in those countries where the knowledge of one or more foreign languages is regarded very favourably and those where it is regarded with indifference or even hostility, it is clear that social and cultural attitudes have a very deep influence on individual learners. A teacher, therefore, may be aided or hindered by factors quite beyond his own control. If social attitudes are negative, the overall achievement can be relatively poor no matter how well he does his job. If social attitudes are positive, learning may proceed even where teaching is not particularly efficient. The achievement will be highest where attitudes and teaching together promote effective learning and lowest where attitudes are negative and teaching is weak.

What has been said about foreign languages in general can also be said about an individual foreign language. Attitudes may relate only to one language, the learning of which may be advanced or retarded for much the same reasons as have already been described. Usually for historical and political reasons, particular languages may be regarded with great favour or great hostility. English, for example, is often better learned in those parts of the world where there has been fruitful collaboration for many years than in those countries where the political power of the English-speaking world for more than a century is somewhat resented. Of course many other factors are involved, but it can be difficult for the pupil to make the considerable effort required for learning a language if the society to which he belongs continually expresses critical attitudes about the people who speak that language.

Language learning will also be much influenced by attitudes towards cultural aspects of language. In one sense language cannot be properly learned without familiarity with features of the culture, since language and culture are inextricably connected. On the other hand it is possible to master the linguistic code without at the same time acquiring a knowledge of the literary culture, the way of life and social values of the target-language group or the social and political institutions of that community. There are great differences in the extent to which, in different parts of the world, language learning is taken to mean familiarizing the pupils with features of a different culture as part of the general educative process. In the west European tradition of language teaching it has always been the practice, and it remains so, to relate the language being learned to the cultural context of the native speakers of that language. This view, however, is not universally held. In some places, learning is associated much more with features of the learner's own culture, usually in order to reinforce the individual's sense of his own culture and sometimes from the desire to reject what are considered alien and unacceptable features of the second-language culture. In these cases the aims of language learning are usually expressed in strictly functional terms. Methods of teaching may not be influenced directly by such considerations, but learning objectives cannot be set without regard for these cultural factors, and methods are at least partly dependent on objectives. More obviously, language-teaching materials will reflect attitudes towards the desired cultural context of language learning.

The factors that have just been discussed are closely associated with the status of the target language in the learner's own country. So far we have used the terms *foreign language* and *second language* without distinguishing between the two, but it is common to use the former to refer to the status of a language which is not used for any normal day-to-day social interaction in the country where it is being learned and, by contrast, to use the latter where, without being the native language of any social group in the country, it is none the less used for such purposes as the conduct of commerce, industry, law, administration, politics and education. The distinction is conceptual rather than actual in that most language situations come somewhere between the two extremes, but it is a methodologically significant dimension, since what is done in the language classroom will differ according to whether or not one is providing the learner with all the language contact that he is going to get.

In the second-language situation, especially if the target language is used as the medium for the teaching of other subjects, the learner will be able, indeed obliged, to use the language while he is in the process of learning it. This gives him an advantage over the foreign-language learner. It is also very likely that the age at which the individual begins to learn the language will be more determined by the status of the language than by any other factor. The proficiency reached in second-language learning should be much higher, and as a result the more advanced stages of language learning should resemble more closely the teaching of the mother-tongue than is likely to be the case in most foreign-language learning situations. The most advantageous learning situation of all should be that of the immigrant, who is a member of a minority language group which is surrounded by a community whose language he needs to learn. He has ample opportunity to use the language he is learning. Indeed, he is frequently obliged to do so. Other factors being equal, he should be able to learn rapidly and reach a higher level of proficiency than either the foreign- or the second-language learner. In fact there are very large differences in the success of different kinds of immigrant community in learning the language of the host community and, in part, this can be accounted for in terms of some of the other factors discussed in this chapter.

While on the subject of social and cultural factors, it should not be forgotten that the learning of languages is not immune from factors that influence other kinds of learning. For example, it has been shown that in the school system, success in language learning, like success in the learning of other subjects on the school curriculum, relates closely to the learners' social background. It has sometimes been argued that since language learning requires a different kind of ability from that needed for other subjects, it offers the chance of academic success to children who do not do well in other subjects.

Research into the learning of French by young children shows that it is the children of white-collar and middle-class parents who have the greatest chance of success and the children of blue-collar parents who have the least. Obviously the adoption by the teacher of a uniform approach to language teaching will not ensure a uniform level of achievement. If all his pupils are to be successful in language learning, he must adopt methods that are sufficiently flexible to provide for the strengths and weaknesses of different types of learner.

3.4 The pupil

Probably the largest variable of all in the learning situation is the pupil himself. In fact many of his qualities have been considered as general characteristics of learners—age, motivation and aptitude, for example—and many more are the product of the social and cultural factors that we have just been discussing. There are, however, one or two further factors that may influence pupils' learning and thereby the way in which the teacher will choose to teach them. In particular, there is the matter of their previous language-learning experience. Of course, any teacher other than one faced with a class of total beginners needs to establish how much of the target language they already know. Within an institution it is usually fairly well established what they ought to know, at least. Faced with learners who are returning to the task of acquiring a language, perhaps after a space of some years, the teacher has a number of problems. If they are returning to learn a language which they have previously been taught, there is the fact that they have, presumably, not been entirely successful in the previous learning. Will the teacher, therefore, simply repeat what was taught before in much the same way as it was taught before? Would this not be to guarantee failure for a second time, since the learners would be faced with precisely the same difficulties that they had not been able to overcome the first time? He might prefer to activate what knowledge they have, to eradicate their incorrect learning and to extend their knowledge further by adopting different organization and different methods so that the learning experience is a new and fresh one.

In doing this the teacher could encounter a problem that he might also find if he was teaching a totally new language to pupils who had previous experience in learning another language. The earlier experience will have given the pupils expectations about the way in which languages should and should not be taught. Contrary to what might be anticipated, students who may not have been all that successful in learning a language none the less often expect to be taught in the manner with which they are familiar. There is considerable danger in overriding the pupil's expectations, since it risks creating a hostility towards the teacher that would seriously interfere with the pupil's ability to learn. The hostility might be increased if the learners thought that the methods adopted were not appropriate to their age or status, as could be the case with many modern methods. The teacher, therefore, is faced with the choice of convincing his pupils that what he wants to do is indeed in their own best interests, or of modifying what he would like to do in the direction of what his pupils expect of him. Whichever path he adopts, the important thing is that he should not lose the sympathy of his pupils. He needs to have them working with him, not against him.

He is in any case more likely to have this sympathy if the learners have chosen freely to learn the language. Within educational systems this is rarely the case. The language is often just one part of a compulsory curriculum. This means that none of the learners has actually chosen to learn the language, and it is perhaps the case that few of them would have chosen to if they had been given the choice. This can mean that the majority of a class may have little intrinsic interest in language learning. When a class consists of voluntary learners a certain degree of self-motivation can be taken for granted and exploited, but when learners are not volunteers, the teacher must himself stimulate and sustain motivation. The methodological implications of this are considerable, since for many learners some methods and techniques will be much more readily motivating than others. The benefits of language learning may need to be kept continually self-evident and there may need to be a strong element of play, humour and entertainment. Weakly-motivated learners, by definition, have difficulty in recognizing long-term benefits and need to find the learning process itself an interesting one.

Lack of motivation goes hand-in-hand with hostile attitudes towards members of other language communities. We have seen that individual attitudes may be culturally conditioned, but in discussing this we have been concerned with attributes of the learning group as a whole. Over and above this there may be considerable differences in the attitudes of individual pupils. Research has shown that where learners have rigid, ethnocentric and authoritarian views, not surprisingly they are less successful in language learning. Other races, nationalities or language groups may be regarded as unreliable, unclean, undisciplined, too emotional, too reserved, uncultured, physically weak, lazy, too formal or dishonest. Particularly interesting is the fact that the attitudes of children are almost always the attitudes of their parents also, so that it could be said that the parents do much to determine the lack of success of their children in learning a foreign language. The existence of such pupils presumably adds strength to the general educational arguments for the teaching of foreign languages in a rich cultural context.

3.5 The teacher

The one remaining important variable in the learning situation is the teacher himself. His skill and his personality are instrumental in creating the conditions for learning. His skill is dependent on two factors, his own proficiency in the language and his knowledge of and expertise in methods and techniques of language teaching. The language proficiency of teachers cannot be taken for granted. There are countries where the teachers themselves have been relatively ill taught, where resources are lacking, so that teachers will never have the opportunity to visit the country where the language they teach is spoken, where the education system itself is relatively undeveloped and where teachers consequently are hardly able themselves to use the language for real communication. By contrast, in countries where there is a long tradition of language learning and where adequate resources have long been devoted to education and to language teaching, teachers will usually be able to use the language with fluency and accuracy. This is not to deny that there will, in any situation, be considerable differences between individual teachers. What the teachers are able to achieve will be limited to what their own command of language permits. Even with modern aids available it is the teacher's language which remains the principal model for the pupil. The best that can be expected is that the pupils' achievement will fall somewhat short of the target set by the teacher in the form of his own skill in the language. It would be unrealistic to expect a teacher to set objectives which he himself is not capable of reaching. A teacher who himself has difficulty in speaking the language he teaches is not going to succeed in giving his pupils a command of spoken language. Objectives, therefore, have to be set realistically in the light of the teacher's own skill in the language.

Much the same is true of teaching methods. Different methods demand different linguistic skills from the teacher. Some can only be used by teachers who have great confidence and facility in their use of the language. Much modern teaching places very great demands on a teacher's oral command of language. If there are teachers who have never had the opportunity to develop the necessary command, there would be little point in obliging them to use methods which presuppose a language proficiency which they do not possess. This would ensure that teaching was unsatisfactory and the results could well be worse than if more modest but practicable methods were adopted.

The other aspect of the teacher's professional skill is his understanding of language and language learning and his command of methods and techniques of language teaching. Here too, what can be expected of any individual teacher is constrained by his or her level of expertise. This is particularly important at a time of considerable methodological innovation. Teachers cannot be expected to put new methods into practice effectively unless they are thoroughly familiar with both the principles and the details of the methods. Too hasty a change may do no more than guarantee that what is done is badly done, and the disappointing results that will inevitably ensue will only discredit methods that have not in fact been given a fair trial. It is probably true to say that modern methods require more careful preparation and a greater display of pedagogic skills than more conventional methods. The majority of teachers have never been trained in these methods. It is not realistic nor ultimately desirable to expect that they will happily and efficiently change their approach to language teaching overnight.

The need for the best possible professional preparation of language teachers is self-evident, but that is a matter of long-term educational planning and is not the issue here. What pupils learn cannot go beyond what their teachers are able to present to them. Faced with immediate decisions about objectives and the methods by which they might be reached, the teacher must be aware of the limits of his own expertise. In a more centralized educational system, where teachers are not left free to make their own decisions, requirements must be based on a realistic appreciation of the present qualities of teachers. If then it is thought desirable that new syllabuses should be set up and new methods adopted, it should only be done in conjunction with a programme of retraining. In short, the qualities of language teachers define the potential limits of achievement of their pupils.

The success of an individual teacher is by no means entirely a matter of his degree of professional training. He brings with him certain important personality characteristics that can go a long way towards determining whether his pupils make the most of their opportunities for learning. If he has an inherent sensitivity to other people, he will gain the sympathy of his pupils, he will be immediately conscious of their success or failure to learn from the language context that he is creating for them and, as a result, he will adopt an intuitive flexibility that so often distinguishes the good teacher. If, on the other hand, he is insensitive, authoritarian and rigid, his pupils will learn less happily and less efficiently from him. Unfortunately, a change of personality is not often one of the products of the training of teachers and although it is certainly one of the factors that affects learning, it is not one that can easily be taken into account in devising a set of methodological principles.

E

4 *Methodological principles of foreign-language teaching*

4.1 Introduction

In the Prologue it was suggested that it is naïve to believe it possible to decide what is *the* best method of foreign-language teaching. The preceding three chapters have shown why this is so. A multiplicity of linguistic, psychological and environmental factors act upon the process of language learning. There is no way of giving a precise weighting to the importance of these different factors. On the contrary the relationship between them may vary according to circumstances, so that a factor that has a powerful effect on learning in one case may have virtually no effect in another. We are far from having sufficiently reliable knowledge about any one of the factors involved to be able, for example, to build a computer model of language learning which could be trusted to give a reasonably accurate prediction of actual learning behaviour. It is desirable that research should continue in an effort to reach that level of knowledge, but it must for the present be regarded as a distinctly long-term objective. For us to conclude that there was a single method suitable for all occasions, we would have to be certain of the contribution of all possible factors to learning and we would have to reject the possibility of inherent variability in the relationship between them. What is more, we would have to deny that the objectives of learning were in any way relevant to the question of what might be the most efficient methods by which the objectives could be reached. Yet, as we shall see, the consequence of this is that objectives tend to be tailored to methods instead of methods to objectives. This hardly seems to be in the learner's best interests.

To suggest that it is not possible to arrive at exact methodological and linguistic programming of general validity is not to suggest that no methodological decisions can be taken at all. The language teacher has to decide what procedures he will follow and how his course will be structured. As we have seen, he has many things to bear in mind. Whatever his eventual conclusions, he cannot decide *a priori* that the audiovisual, the audiolingual, the structural, the grammar-translation or whatever other method is the one that he must use. In fact it is not certain that it matters very much which 'method' he adopts as the basis of his teaching. A closer look at this apparent paradox may help us to understand what kind of principles underlie language learning.

If we look at all widely at the practice of language teaching, we will see that pupils may develop much the same level and kind of language command in spite of the fact that their teachers have, within limits, used different methods. If we are honest with ourselves, we will admit that some pupils at least have in the past learned by means of methods that we commonly castigate as 'bad', and equally that the use of more favourably-regarded methods does not necessarily ensure learning. The only conclusion that can be drawn from this is that the method, in the sense of a set of materials organized into a fixed pedagogic sequence, requiring the use of classroom techniques which embody a certain view of language learning, is not the sole determinant of language learning. It is possible for the same aims to be reached by different paths. There are two reasons why this is so. In the first place, when we say that a teacher is using a certain method, we are only giving a very superficial account of the actual language experience that he is providing for his pupils. We focus on the most obvious features of his methods and techniques, where a closer examination of what he actually does in the classroom may reveal that he adds to or subtracts from what the method requires in ways that could be either beneficial or detrimental to learning. Most methods carry within them the seeds of distortion and may be applied in ways that contradict the possible benefits that they offer to the learner.

Secondly, it may be the case that the differences between methods are less significant than the similarities. In comparing methods we tend to contrast them, paying most attention to the differences, whereas, viewed more deeply, they may have a good deal in common. A teacher may use some techniques of which we would disapprove, but if they are part of a general teaching strategy that creates the optimum conditions for learning, they may in no way hinder learning. Conversely, the benefits of what is potentially sound in a method may be lost if the overall approach to language teaching is defective. Provided the method he adopts permits the teacher to do certain things well, he will be as successful as our present understanding of language and learning allows. In my view there are only three principles upon which one needs to insist, although there are other less significant factors which can also be exploited in order to promote learning. It is because these principles are few in number and broad in scope that it is possible for there to be underlying similarities in orms of teaching that contrast in their more superficial details. This in turn explains how it is that 'different' methods may prove equally successful in practice and how 'the same' methods may result in different levels of achievement. The remainder of the discussion is devoted to consideration first of the three general principles and secondly of certain other factors that arise from our knowledge of language and learning.

4.2 First principle: objectives to be clearly defined

The basis of a sound approach to language teaching is to know what the objectives of teaching are. There are no immutable and ideal objectives in language teaching. Objectives are set in relation to the particular teaching situation with which the teacher is faced. This means that, as far as circumstances allow, it is necessary to predict what kinds of language skill will be of greatest value to the learners. We have already noted that objectives cannot be set without regard for any limitations that the learning situation imposes. The skill of the teachers, the size of the classes, the time available and many other factors have to be taken into account in the framing of the objectives. The precise linguistic implications of the objectives set must also be understood. For the pupil to have certain kinds of linguistic behaviour under his control, what knowledge of the grammatical system, the sociolinguistic system, the lexical and the phonological system is necessary? It is not likely that the teacher will be able to instil the practical linguistic knowledge that underlies actual language behaviour if he is not aware of the components of that knowledge.

If we look at the whole spectrum of situations in which languages are taught, we will see that there is great variation in the degree to which we can predict the future language needs of groups of learners. The precise purposes for which somebody wants to learn a language may be known and a very detailed and narrow analysis of what is wanted can be produced. The target could be a skill in language in a very specialized field, or a very limited level of general achievement in the language. Most teachers, working within school systems, face a situation where accurate prediction of future language needs is scarcely possible. In that case the teacher has to make certain assumptions about what will be of greatest general value to his pupils. The fact that precise behavioural predictions are not possible does not mean that the teacher himself should not have thought carefully about what his objectives in teaching the language are. He may be forced to express them in the most general terms, but they are no less valuable for that. He cannot logically take decisions about methods if he does not first know what the methods are intended to achieve.

4.3 Second principle: learning activities to be representative of learning objectives

When objectives have been defined, the most important single methodological principle is to ensure that the linguistic and learning experience is planned so as to be completely representative of the objectives and of the different components of those objectives. This formulation sounds rather abstract and vague, but its implications are practical and far-reaching. It reflects the essential truth of the behaviourist view that 'we learn what we do', while not insisting on too narrow an interpretation of *do*. We cannot learn what we have not experienced. We learn something roughly in proportion to the degree of experience that we have of it. That being so, the teacher should provide a learning experience for his pupils that reflects the proportions of the objectives that he has already established. If some part of the objectives is not present in his contact with the language, his achievement will be deficient to that extent. Since the objectives themselves will be definable partly in terms of the components of language that were discussed in the first chapter, we can judge any proposed methods by how far they cover these components. One reason why methods tend to have different strengths and weaknesses is that they tend to emphasize different aspects of the linguistic code. Individual teachers who make good these deficiencies may still be successful. Hence it is possible for the same aims to be reached by different approaches. In making such judgements it is the language-learning experience as a whole that needs to be considered, not the situation at any one point in the learning programme. One course may begin with a heavy dominance of written language, another with spoken; one course may work with individual sentences, another with dialogues; one course may be more meaningful, another more formal in the early stages; one course may insist at the beginning on productive activities, another on receptive. Methods and materials can differ on many dimensions, but what they contribute to learning depends on what they contain in their totality and not just on how they begin or end. This makes possible almost an infinity of possible arrangements, which could, none the less, ultimately add up to much the same whole.

This 'principle of representative proportions' has important implications for the balance of the four language activities (more conventionally, four language skills) of speaking, understanding speech, writing and reading. The relative place of these four activities is always one of the most important methodological questions. Our principle requires that the quantity of each activity in the classroom should reflect its place in the overall objectives. If we have to enable our pupils above all to read and write the language, most of the contact hours will be devoted to actual reading and writing. If their need is only for listening comprehension, then their time should be spent in listening, not in reading, writing or speaking. In the general language courses that are typically taught in schools, however, statements of objectives cannot be based on exact behavioural predictions, so that some uncertainty surrounds both the objectives and the methods for reaching them. Since the four language activities break down further into two pairs of oppositions, speech versus writing and production versus reception, we can consider whether there is any case for giving prominence to any one of these four dimensions in either the objectives or the methods of language teaching.

4.3.1 *Speech and writing: objectives*

Are there then any arguments for believing that either speech or writing is a better or more proper objective in language teaching, particularly in the context of a general language course? In recent years it has been argued on both linguistic and psychological grounds that spoken language should be the principal objective in language teaching. For various reasons the linguist has concluded that speech is the primary form of language and that writing is secondary to it and derived from it. For not dissimilar reasons—man learns to speak but not necessarily to write, the child *learns* to speak but is *taught* to write—psychologists have come to the same conclusion. As a result the study of language has focused very much on speech. Sometimes explicitly, sometimes implicitly under the influence of these views methodologists have argued that speech should be the main aim of language teaching. Yet, whatever other arguments there are, there seems no reason why the significance of speech to the linguist and the psychologist should be thought in any way relevant to the definition of language-teaching aims. Looked at historically, linguistics played its part in ensuring that speech was not regarded as some inferior form of language when compared with writing, and to that extent it has helped make it possible for speech to be accepted as a respectable goal in language learning. But language teaching exists for the benefit of the learner, and in a situation of low predictability there is no reason to think that the spoken language will be any more useful to him than the written.

There are at least two other arguments that can be used to support the view that greater prominence should be given to speech. There is the possibility that pupils may be more motivated to learn spoken than written language. Where they lack intrinsic motivation, the fact that language is a means of day-to-day communication needs to be kept continually before them, and this can perhaps be more easily appreciated if the language is in its spoken form. In practice most learners are no more likely to be engaged in spoken than in written communication, although many young people who learn English as a foreign language are happy to be able to understand British and American pop music. None the less, being able to speak the foreign language makes it more like their mother-tongue which they more often speak than write. Whether or not motivation can be significantly affected in this way, it does show that a factor in learning which in some situations is of little importance can in another situation possibly develop overriding importance.

The other argument links methodology and objectives. It is that a knowledge of spoken language is more easily transferred to the written medium than the converse. At a subjective level this reflects the difficulties in speaking the language that have been experienced by learners taught by largely traditional writing-based methods. At another level it can be traced to the rather simplistic views held by some linguists that writing is no more than the graphic representation of spoken language. The result of these arguments has tended to be that a far larger proportion of the teaching time in recent years has been devoted to speech, in the belief that the learner himself with some assistance could make the transfer to writing. Since, in practice, the learning of language in either medium needs to be provided for by specific teaching, as is witnessed by the fact that children spend so much time learning to write their mother-tongue, the achievement has usually been a higher proficiency in speech than in writing. In this case the emphasis in the methods had, and still has, the effect of modifying the potential achievement and effectively, therefore, the objectives. In fact, the bias towards writing could have been corrected without a compensating bias towards speech. A proper balance between the two was all that was needed.

4.3.2 *Speech and writing: methods*

Whatever their differences, all methods of language teaching developed and adopted in recent years can be called *oral* methods. They are oral either in that they insist on an initial period of learning, lasting from anything from one month to two years, in which contact with the written language is entirely withheld, or in that they require all new pieces of linguistic form to be first presented and then practised in the spoken medium with little or no use of the written form as a stimulus. Quite often a method is oral in both these senses. Obviously in so far as such a methodological principle is simply a reflection of a new emphasis on speech in the overall objectives, it loses its validity if it can be shown that speech is no more important an objective than writing. Very often however, it is suggested that the methods should be oral even where the objectives are no less to write than to speak the language. Support for this view is found in the facts that in language acquisition speech precedes writing and that, linguistically, writing is derived from speech. We saw that this piece of evidence from language acquisition cannot be considered valid when applied to language learning. The linguistic argument is no more sound. To suggest that writing either should or can only be developed on the basis of a prior knowledge of speech is contradicted by the argument often used against traditional methods, namely that they teach a satisfactory reading and writing knowledge without developing a command of spoken language. Provided the orthography is familiar (that is to say, some phonological interpretation can be put on the writing system, even if it is not a particularly accurate one), reading and writing can be developed with a minimal speaking knowledge.

Whether there is any advantage to a particular ordering of speech and writing or to a particular balance of the two is a pragmatic question. Is there any arrangement that is simply more efficient than all others? There is no direct evidence to suggest that this is so. A good deal of research intended to compare different teaching methods has produced largely inconclusive results. Apparently contrasting methods do not produce significant differences in type and level of achievement, though there is some tendency for the dominant language activity in the teaching programme to be reflected in a higher performance in that activity. Not too much should be made of the significance of the language-teaching research that has been conducted so far, but it does nothing to contradict the argument being put forward here.

It would be a relevant consideration if it could be shown that speech was intrinsically more difficult than writing. If the objective is an equivalent attainment in the two forms of language, this would mean a greater investment of learning effort in speech. Alternatively it could lead to a modification of objectives, since there is much to be said for concentrating learning upon what is most easily acquired. In some situations learners have relevant language knowledge even before they start to learn the foreign language. If they are literate in their own language and that language uses the Latin orthography, for example, they are already part of the way towards their objectives in reading and writing a foreign language which makes use of the same orthography. What may be important is that contact with spoken language in most situations can only be provided in the classroom, whereas experience of written language can be built up extensively outside normal lessons. In this case, though the method as a whole does not have a bias towards speech, the classroom activity does. But for the learner to be able to take advantage of this possibility he needs sufficient knowledge of written language, and this can only be instilled in the classroom. Deliberate teaching of written language is, therefore, something that should not be delayed.

Ultimately it probably matters little how speech and writing are ordered in relation to one another. The nature of the language skills developed by learners will depend on how much of their language experience is oral and how much is written, not on the position of the two in the sequence of the language-teaching programme. Since research does show that linguistic forms that are seen (or seen and heard) are more easily learned than those that are only heard, there is every reason for arguing that once the phonological system of the target language is established with tolerable accuracy every effort should be made to associate spoken and written symbol in the learning process. Purely oral practice will, of course, still be necessary, but there is no justification for giving long-term priority to spoken language in one's teaching method. A course in which the early stages were predominantly written and the later stages extensively spoken could probably have the same results as one in which the ordering was reversed.

4.3.3 *Production and reception: objectives*

The second opposition was that of language production and language reception. Again the question can be asked whether there is any reason for giving prominence to either as an objective or within the method. If we continue to limit our consideration to the general language learner, we will conclude that both aspects of language are important for him, but in saying this we should not assume that it means that what the learner knows for production should be exactly the same as what he knows for reception. Such a state of affairs would not in any way reflect the facts of our normal language behaviour. The language that we understand in reading and listening in our mother-tongue is grammatically and lexically far more diverse than the language that we ourselves produce or, in some cases, than the language that we are even capable of producing. It would be quite unrealistic and unnatural to expect that our knowledge of a foreign language should for some reason be different in this respect.

We saw too that in language acquisition the child's comprehension precedes and exceeds his productive capacity, so that it is significantly easier to learn to understand language than to produce it. In formulating the objectives of language learning both these facts should be borne in mind. Through developing the pupils' understanding of language, we can give them a rapid sense of achievement in language learning and we can do it, given the relative ease with which comprehension develops, with less rigorous programming of learning than is necessary for the development of productive abilities. There is no reason, therefore, for under-emphasizing the importance and usefulness of receptive language abilities in defining the objectives of language learning and teaching.

4.3.4. Production and reception: methods

Interestingly, modern methods are notably alike in the extent to which they require the productive participation of the learner in the learning process. This stems partly from a reaction against the somewhat passive role of the learner in traditional teaching, but more from the belief that learning only takes place when the learner himself is active. Since, at the same time, receptive abilities are erroneously thought of as passive, the demand for active participation becomes a demand for the learner to engage principally in the production of language. Materials are planned so that each newly-introduced linguistic form, be it a grammatical structure or a lexical item, is thoroughly practised by the learner. *Practised* here means that he himself is given repeated opportunities to produce the form—orally, because of the simultaneous emphasis on speech. To make this possible there is a strict limit on the number of new forms in any learning unit, so that the burden of what must be covered productively is not too great. It is often the case that everything that is learned at what may be roughly labelled the elementary and intermediate levels is learned for production.

As might be expected, the results of this productive emphasis in the method will be a strengthening of productive skills and a weakening of the receptive skills, although it should not be forgotten that the exact nature of the achievement will depend on the exact nature of the experience. As we shall see in the next section, even intensive oral practice may not provide all that is necessary for a mastery of spontaneous oral production.

There are two reservations about the role given in current language teaching to productive language activities. First, all language knowledge is tied to what there is time to produce in the classroom. We have already seen that this does not reflect in any way either the normal balance of our language knowledge or the relationship between production and comprehension in language acquisition. This constraint is quite unnecessarily and damagingly artificial. The fact that comprehension can develop ahead of production is something that should be recognized and exploited in language teaching. As it is, it tends to be suppressed in the belief that it is confusing for the learner to be in contact with forms that are not fully within his productive repertoire. Since this is an inevitable part of anyone's day-to-day language experience, it is better that the learner should be prepared for it.

The second reservation is that limiting the learning experience to production guarantees a very slow and thin exposure to language. We saw that language acquisition is based on a rich, varied and intensive contact with language. In language learning the time available for contact is already considerably reduced. If we insist too much on language production, because this requires maximal repetition of specific linguistic forms, we offer a still weaker exposure to language even within the learning time available. If we give a larger place to receptive activities, not only do we ensure that the receptive abilities themselves are better learned, we give the learner the opportunity to learn what is not taught. In language learning a rich exposure to language can only be provided through extensive reading and listening. The transfer of linguistic knowledge from receptive to productive repertoires is probably a relatively slow process, but it does take place, as the study of language acquisitions shows. There are good linguistic reasons why in teaching we should do our utmost to take advantage of the wider exposure that reading and listening activities offer.

The nature of linguistic meaning is such that the acquisition of meaning is a continuing process. Since it is the product of highly complex networks of relationships between linguistic items, it can be learned only if the language is experienced sufficiently for those networks to be built up in the learner. The networks of associations developed in coursebooks and in readers which are structurally and lexically tied to the accompanying textbooks fall far short of those that the native speaker is aware of. This is, of course, a target that no foreign-language learner can hope to reach, but an adequate knowledge of semantic systems even for the language learner requires a good deal more than the textbook usually provides. The planned content of the textbook cannot give him a knowledge of collocational restrictions in the language either. This is something that is better learned through wide exposure.

Syntactic knowledge cannot be built up fully through step-by-step productive procedures. In the usual approach individual linguistic structures are progressively accumulated. Without there being any need to question this approach at this point, since the number of actual sentence structures in a language is potentially infinite, they could not all be enumerated in any course and could not be acquired by a simple additive process. The structural content of the first years of language courses certainly does not include all the possible structures in the language. Learners must have the opportunity to learn those aspects of syntactic structure which are not explicitly taught. If their syntactic experience is limited to what the coursebook provides, there will be a severe limitation in their capacity to exploit the grammatical system of the language. By being exposed through reading and listening to language whose linguistic content is not kept wholly within what the productive syllabus contains, they can gradually build up this wider syntactic knowledge. Given that learners do possess some capacity for recognizing in other people's language performance linguistic information that is relevant to their own learning of the language, reading and listening are a useful source of feedback for the learner. They provide him with continuing information about the grammatical systems with which he is already partly familiar.

One may thus conclude that receptive learning activities are more beneficial than is commonly allowed. Reading is the more easily planned of the two receptive activities. In most languages there is a wealth of reading material available. Initially, simplified and structurally-controlled readers can be used so that sound reading practices are inculcated, but there is no need to insist that the linguistic content of readers should in no way go beyond that of the general coursebook. The reading materials used can move progressively towards texts which have been produced for the native speaker and are not specially edited for the language learner. If the texts are not narrowly literary, as in much more traditional language teaching, and have been drawn from a wide variety of types of writing, the learner will simultaneously be acquiring some of the distinctive characteristics of stylistic and sociolinguistic variation. Once sufficient classroom time has been devoted to reading to establish a sound pattern of reading technique, the major portion of reading can be done out of class time, so that effectively encouraging reading is one way of increasing the pupil's language contact time.

Listening presents rather greater problems. Any productive classroom activity almost inevitably demands some listening activity too. However, what the pupil hears is scarcely language in use for communication. One would not easily take classroom language for natural language use. Furthermore, much of it is produced either by the teacher or by other pupils. Learners are rarely used to the sound of the language spoken by native speakers and consequently have problems of understanding when they do hear native speakers. Anyway, what the teacher says is usually controlled in just the way that would prevent listening from providing the rich linguistic exposure that one is seeking. Where the resources are available the teacher can provide what is needed through film, tape, radio or record, but this is probably better kept within the classroom until the learner has reached advanced stages of learning. A few courses do plan listening experience that goes beyond what is being taught productively, and perhaps more thought should be given to this.

The general conclusion to be reached on the role of the four language activities is that where objectives are of some fairly specialized kind, the distribution of the activities in the teaching programme should reflect their distribution in the objectives. A reading knowledge is best acquired by doing lots of reading, a writing knowledge by doing lots of writing, a speaking knowledge by doing lots of speaking and so on. Where courses are making a more general language provision, there seems no reason to exaggerate one activity to the detriment of the others, nor will it matter significantly how the different activities are ordered in relation to one another.

4.4 Third principle: learners to model their own language performance on significant instances of target-language behaviour

Language learning will proceed more efficiently if specific instances of language behaviour are modelled for the learner and if he is given ample opportunity to engage in analogous behaviour

based on the model provided. If he is learning language for productive use, this means that he must himself produce further instances
of the same type of language behaviour. If he is learning language for
receptive use, his comprehension of the model and of other examples
of what is represented in the model must be ensured. The need for
this lies quite simply in the different conditions under which
language learning and language acquisition take place. We are
concerned as teachers with encouraging the language-learning
processes to operate as efficiently as possible. If we were to leave
the learning of the language system to the operation of inductive
processes on a random experience of language, the paucity of the
contact and the lack of intensity would result in a superficial and
low level of achievement. By isolating and focusing on particular
pieces of language we aim to short-cut the inductive learning process.

The pieces of language on which the learner is to model his own
behaviour should always represent significant generalizations about
the structure of the language. If the forms cannot be widely general-
ized, there is less benefit to the learner in acquiring them. Utterances, sentences, phrases are not set up to be learned in themselves.
Such learning would be the straightforward memorization of
formulae, as in a phrasebook, and language learning should be
learning to construct and create sentences. The object of providing
a piece of language as a sample is that it illustrates some significant
part of the linguistic system at work, but it is the linguistic system,
or the part of it concerned, that the learner must master, not the
sample itself. It is through this process of the learner basing his own
linguistic behaviour analogously on given samples that he acquires
the finite linguistic rules from which he can produce the infinity of
utterances. Most commonly, and rightly, it is the grammatical
system that is learned in this way: but the generalizations could
equally well represent significant facts of stylistic or sociolinguistic
use. They could demonstrate important ways in which the grammatical system is exploited in actual acts of communication, or could
focus on distinctive characteristics of the phonological system.

What is learned should be much more than what is actually
taught, in the sense that the learner is mastering rules that are to be
applied in far more cases than those which he will actually produce

or observe within the pedagogic units. From a limited number of examples of singular and plural nouns, the learner will acquire knowledge of general rules of plural formation, which will be valid for most if not all of the nouns which he has not yet met. This is why coursebooks and syllabuses, whatever their linguistic and methodological orientation, are so similar in content over the first years of learning. They concentrate on the most general aspects of language structure, those where the largest amount of learning can be expected for a given quantity of teaching. To assist the learner's sense of the generalizability of what he is learning, it is important that he should be able to see that it has linguistic value beyond the immediate learning context. To learn forms only for particular contexts is again likely to prove to be a kind of phrasebook learning, producing 'language-like behaviour' rather than true language.

Provided the language modelled for the learner is formally correct and meaningful to him, it probably does not matter precisely in what form it is presented. It needs to be formally correct so that the learner's own behaviour has every chance of being correctly formed. It needs to be fully meaningful, not only so that grammatical meaning as well as grammatical form is being acquired, but so that the learner has a sense of the deeper structural relationships within the sentence. If pieces of language are presented as forms devoid of meaning, there is no way in which the learner can know what the grammatical forms signify nor, in some cases, can he know the exact nature of the grammatical devices themselves, unless, that is, he makes assumptions based on his knowledge of his mother-tongue. These may or may not prove correct. Even the operation of a device as apparently simple as word-order cannot be entirely clear to a learner if he does not understand the meaning of the sentence as a whole. We should not forget either the psychological evidence that language is learned better when it is meaningful to the learner. There seems little to be said for deliberately engaging the language learner in meaningless activity.

The model pieces of language set up for the learner may be in the form of individual sentences, dialogues (either structurally controlled or more heterogeneous), texts (either written or spoken),

F

or, in more traditional teaching, paradigms. In all except the latter case, the pieces of language are potentially 'instances of language behaviour'. Paradigms are above all aids to memorization and are probably more valuable in this role than we have been prepared to admit, but they are not instances of language behaviour because they are made up of linguistic forms isolated from the wider structural context in which they must naturally occur. Paradigms, therefore, are not adequate as models for the learner's own language behaviour. With any of the other approaches to the presentation of language, the piece of language that is isolated for him will be not less than a sentence. As a result it will have a certain grammatical and semantic completeness that makes it a suitable model for language learning.

When the teacher is deciding which pieces of language he will set up as models for his pupils, he must bear in mind the limitations imposed by their short-term memory. In the early stages of language learning, when their proficiency has not yet developed very far, they will be able to store only relatively short and simple linguistic structures. If the teacher selects sentences which exceed the capacity of their short-term memory, he will induce error. Since the most useful linguistic forms are not necessarily the most simple, some of the linguistic generalizations that on other grounds one might want a learner to make early on in his language learning will have to be deferred until his general proficiency has reached the point where his short-term memory can cope with the more complex structures.

The teacher also needs to ensure that contact with forms learned is maintained. However intensively they have worked to learn a linguistic form, pupils will not retain what they have learned if that form subsequently disappears from their linguistic experience for some considerable time. One of the improvements in course design in recent years has been the care that writers have taken to ensure the regular recurrence of forms once they have been taught.

There are broadly two strategies for setting up the samples on which the learner is to base his own language behaviour. We can either begin with the language broken down into component parts, which are ordered into a pedagogic sequence and fed to the learner one at a time. The learner gradually builds up his store of language.

New language always occurs in the context of language that is already familiar. The possible range and variety of language in actual use is only met relatively late in the learning sequence. This is by far the most commonly adopted approach to language teaching. In modern methods the new language either occurs in a succession of structurally analogous but contextually-unrelated sentences, or it is embedded in a specially-written dialogue. In audiolingual language teaching a new grammatical structure is usually first presented to the learner in a specially-written dialogue. The dialogue, which is normally very short, provides a context for the new structure and the pupil can learn to use it as a response to another sentence with which he will probably be familiar from previous lessons. Subsequently, the new structure is taken out of the dialogue and through structural drills (pattern practice) the pupil is given intensive opportunity to produce further sentences, identical in structure but varied in vocabulary. In structural or situational language teaching, the new structure tends to be produced initially as an isolated sentence, which is associated with features of the classroom context so that its meaning becomes clear. As in audiolingual teaching, practice takes the form of intensive oral production of further sentences having identical structure to the one that was presented initially. However, whereas in audiolingual teaching the practice is cued verbally, by use of such techniques as substitution, insertion, expansion and transformation, in situational teaching the cues are usually visual. The teacher manipulates the physical situation or makes use of visual aids as cues for intensive oral production. There is no reason why longer spoken and written texts should not be used, so long as the language within them is carefully controlled, but this is not often done.

The alternative approach would be to let the learner meet a much greater variety of linguistic forms from the beginning, possibly even language that had not been specially prepared for the learner, and then to focus only on one or more specific parts of the text for the modelling process to take place. In this case by no means all the language that is encountered by the learner is subjected to techniques that are intended to encourage the process of generalization. The nearest approach to this in a modern method is found in audiovisual language teaching. The approach resembles audiolingual teaching only in so far as the initial presentation of new language is in the form of a dialogue. But the dialogue, although specially constructed, is intended to resemble a natural conversation much more accurately. It is longer and may contain several new linguistic items. It will inevitably be more varied linguistically. As with situational teaching, a context is provided for the dialogue, usually in the form of a sequence of pictures, each illustrating one of the utterances in the dialogue. The practice that is intended to promote inductive generalizations again involves taking some of the language structures out of their original dialogue context, but instead of having the analogous production based simply on other examples of the very sentence structure that is being learned, it is cued by such processes as question and answer so that the closer resemblance to natural language production remains.

Whereas the former approach, which begins with separate units of language and gradually accumulates them into the larger whole, might be thought of as essentially *synthetic*, the latter, in which the process is reversed, might be termed *analytic*. While the two are conceptually distinct, it is possible for the linguistic organization of learning to be neither fully synthetic nor fully analytic, although much teaching leans fairly clearly in one direction or the other.

There are reasons why an analytic or synthetic approach might be preferred in specific circumstances. For example, where learners are going to need to use the language for real social communication while they are learning it, there will be advantages in basing teaching on an analytic presentation since it permits far greater freedom in the choice of linguistic forms that the learner will meet. On the other hand there are situations (for example where the pupils are young children) where the quantity of unfamiliar language implied in the analytic approach would be quite daunting. In general, however, either approach may lead to successful language learning.

A rather different dimension in consideration of the generalizing process is the possible contribution to learning of making the grammatical generalization explicit. It is possible for learning to be left wholly to the learner's powers of induction. In this case any linguistic rule is left implicit in the samples of language that are repeatedly provided for the learner's benefit. But we saw that many learners may gain from a verbalization of the rule being acquired and it would seem perverse to deny or neglect this. Whether such a grammatical statement should occur initially or at some later point in the modelling process probably matters little. Provided the learner is able to make sense of explicit formulations about the structure of the language he is learning (and this might be a question of age or educational background), his learning will be accelerated by them and the teaching process will be rendered more efficient.

What is certain, though, is that, even where the teacher does give explicit rules, his pupils' effective mastery of the linguistic generalization is dependent less on their conscious understanding of the rule concerned than on the amount of opportunity they have had to apply it in the construction of utterances. If much classroom time is spent in discussion of the linguistic facts of the language, then, following the second methodological principle, what will be learned is the ability to discuss linguistic facts. So, whatever assistance is to be found in more cognitive procedures, in developing a practical command of language it is the number of occasions on which the learner can base his own language behaviour on the models that are provided for him that counts.

There are certain characteristics of this modelling process that are worth commenting on. Inevitably it will begin with largely imitative behaviour. Either there will be exact repetitions of the models set by the teacher or there will be reproductions involving minimal manipulations of the model. However, no matter how intensively this is done it does not create sufficient conditions for language learning. At worst, and based on a very narrow conception of the nature of language, some courses limit the modelling process to imitative and manipulative activities which develop the learner's command of the formal devices of language, but fall a long way short of preparing the learner for total language behaviour. At best the specific instances of language behaviour, and the techniques by which they are exploited, provide a familiarity not only with grammatical form, but with grammatical meaning, stylistic variety and the ways in which the grammatical system of language is exploited in actual utterances. We must not expect the learner to learn more than the linguistic facts which we offer him. If the models are deficient as samples of language, his learning will be equally deficient. But in any case, however well done, the modelling process alone is not enough to bring the learner to the point of linguistic creativity. This is because it is essentially a controlled process. The form of the sentences that the learner repeats or, in a limited way, constructs is determined by the teacher, not the pupil himself. Certain choices may be built in and it is certainly desirable that they should be, but, as long as the activity is model-based, it is artificial, not a true piece of language behaviour.

By devoting a proportion of the language-learning experience to a modelling process that is designed to assist the learner's ability to make inductive generalizations, we are protecting him from the additional burden of having to make his own choices. We have seen why it is necessary to do this, but the learner cannot learn how to construct sentences with no external control imposed unless he is given adequate opportunity to try. As with everything else he will only learn what falls within his experience. If all his language production is controlled from outside, he will hardly be competent to control his own language production. He will not be able to transfer his knowledge from a language-learning situation to a language-using situation. There must therefore be provision for freer use of language by the learner, and it must occupy a fairly substantial proportion of the available learning time. We need to provide consistently throughout the language-learning process occasions on which the learner expresses what he himself wants to express through the forms of language that are available to him at his particular stage of language learning. This may be done with difficulty in the earlier stages of language learning, but it becomes progressively easier to accomplish. There are techniques for bridging the gap between complete control and complete freedom, although more thought needs to be given to devising a richer variety of ways of stimulating free language use in the learner.

In language acquisition the child's own language production plays a significant role. He tries out the inductive generalizations that he has been forming and receives feedback as a consequence of his production. There is no reason to doubt that for the language learner too the free production of language, as well as increasing his fluency and spontaneity in use of the language, actually advances his knowledge of the linguistic system itself. By trying to generalize further the language forms with which he has been made familiar under controlled conditions, as he is bound to do in any freer use of language, he discovers the extent of their generalizability. This will be true as long as he is aware of the acceptability of the forms he produces. This in turn presupposes some mechanism for correction, but there does arise here the problem of the conflicting effects of correction that was discussed in the previous chapter.

The provision of feedback for the learner is an essential part of all stages of learning. While he is at the stage of basing his linguistic behaviour on the model provided by the teacher, there is little by way of actual communication that is taking place. Consequently the feedback is largely in the form of the teacher's acceptance or rejection of the utterances that the learner has produced. If the pupil is working without the presence of a teacher, as in a language laboratory or in some kinds of written work, the materials themselves must be arranged in such a way that the pupil himself can check his success in forming sentences. Only when the pupil is using language for communication can he get feedback in the form in which it occurs in language acquisition. He can judge the success of his use of language by the linguistic and non-linguistic behaviour of the people to whom it is addressed. If he asks someone to do something, his feedback will be provided by whether or not they do it.

One consequence of the linguistic control implicit in the modelling stage of learning is that the greater the extent to which the techniques used are imitative and manipulative, the less the attention of the learner tends to be held by the learning task. This means both that his resources for learning are not fully exploited and that, with part of his attention open to other stimuli, there is the possibility of actual distraction from the learning task. In practice there is commonly boredom in language learning because, in attempting to ensure that the language that the pupils produce is exactly what we want, we make the task a relatively easy one for them. Valid as this may be when the learner is making his first attempts to reproduce the model behaviour, since his learning is better founded on correct than on incorrect forms, it would be better if, subsequently, rather than aiming for correct language production at all costs, we devised language-learning activities which were as demanding as possible on the learner, while still making it more than likely that correct forms would be produced.

It is also probable at this stage that the instances of language behaviour that are provided as models for the learner will be idealized pieces of language in the sense that they will lack any of the factors that influence natural language production. Even in the rare case where the approach has been analytic and the text used has been a piece of natural language, once the specific instance of language behaviour has been isolated, it will be treated more as a sentence of the grammar than as an utterance. This is inevitable and there is no great objection to it. However, it means that the learner's contact is with idealized language, not with the type of language he will meet, if he is placed in a natural communication situation. Given the principle that is now familiar to us, he will only be able to deal with natural language to the extent that he has already been familiarized with it. Therefore, if among our objectives in teaching we include, say, the ability to listen to spoken language with comprehension, we must seek to provide adequate contact with that kind of language as part of our teaching programme. The type of listening that is involved in much classroom teaching, and certainly in the modelling stage of learning, is insufficient to meet such an objective, although of course it has a contribution to make. There is plenty of evidence of the difficulties faced by pupils who have previously met only language processed for learning when they first come into contact with language in use under natural conditions.

At this point it might be as well to recall the facts of language that were discussed in the first chapter and which have been alluded to several times in this discussion. If we assume that the objective of teaching must be to assist the learner to reach some degree and kind of linguistic creativity—the ability to produce and receive newly-created utterances—we have to ensure that the language-learning activities are adequately representative of the components of total language behaviour. This means that in deciding how the modelling process will operate and in determining what it will operate on, we must provide for all major aspects of linguistic structure to be met and for a proper balance between the different aspects of language to have been built up. If we are not sufficiently aware of what language is or have a somewhat biased view of its nature, we will produce a skewed linguistic knowledge in the learners. Between them the pieces of language that we isolate as models must familiarize the learner with the formal grammatical devices of the language, tense, aspect, case, number, gender, word-order, concord and so on, with the grammatical meaning of these devices, with their communicative exploitation, with any sociolinguistic or stylistic restraints on their use and with the phonological means by which they are realized in actual utterance.

Although at any one moment, especially in a synthetic approach, we may focus on only one aspect of language, the total exposure we provide must contain all aspects if we want to attain the objective of a balanced knowledge of the language. The teacher needs a sound understanding of the nature of language in general, and of the language that he is teaching in particular, in order to make sure that the pupil has contact with all that he needs and in the right proportions. Just how much of a language any course or syllabus will actually provide a learner with can be assessed by measuring exactly what it isolates for the sake of the learner's inductive processing against the various components of language as outlined in the first chapter and the descriptive details of the language being taught. Valuable as modern techniques have been in extending the range of devices by which teachers can stimulate oral language production, they are more effective in producing a grammatical than a communicative competence in the language.

4.5 The significance of meaning and the role of the mother-tongue

We have so far been chiefly concerned with the learning and teaching of the structural aspects of language. We must not forget that linguistic forms exist to convey meaning: the learning of meaning systems is no less important than the learning of formal systems. *Meaning* here includes the meaning of grammatical forms, the communicative function of sentences used as utterances and, more obviously, the meaning of individual lexical items. The meaning of a linguistic form can be seen as the sum of the extra-linguistic associations that are built up through the occurrence of the form in certain physical contexts and its evident relation to features of the context. This is as true of grammatical and communicative meaning as it is of lexical meaning. Meaning is also the product of intralinguistic associations. The semantic domain of grammatical and lexical forms is defined by other grammatical and lexical forms. Many linguistic forms cannot be associated with features of the visible, physical world at all, but they are none the less meaningful.

If such is, in very general terms, the nature of meaning, the process of teaching meaning must involve the provision of the necessary linguistic and non-linguistic contexts for these associations to be built up. Where appropriate the modelling process can take place in a physical context which illuminates important semantic features of the linguistic forms involved. Through dramatization and role-playing the communicative function of utterances can be well established. The learning situation can be manipulated to illustrate those aspects of grammatical meaning that have unambiguous situational correlates. Individual lexical items can be associated with relevant objects or representations of them.

Both linguistically and psychologically it is important that the context of presentation should be as rich and varied as possible. For example, to present a lexical item in association with a single object or picture is to do relatively little in establishing the meaning of the word. It invites the learner to overgeneralize the meaning of the word, encouraging, as it does, the idea that there is a clear class of objects, adequately indicated by the one that is shown, and that for this class there is a label in the target language just as there is in the mother-tongue. In the same way as when translation is used to teach meaning, the learner will assume the meaning of the word is the same as the meaning of the equivalent word in the mother-tongue, so that the foreign-language form will become associated with the semantic system of the learner's own language. This is dangerous, since the lexical representation even of common aspects of our everyday physical world varies from language to language. There will be a strong tendency on the part of learners to make this assumption anyway. We can do our best to discourage it by presenting language in a general cultural context that is clearly different from that of the mother-tongue and by establishing a set of visual associations for any item so rich that assumptions of interlingual synonymy will be difficult to sustain. It is also necessary for the learning of any one item that its extralinguistic associations should be contrasted with those of other related items. Without this the limits of its denotation cannot be known.

The learner can only develop the network of intralinguistic relations between linguistic forms in the same way as the native speaker does: by continuing, extensive and varied experience of the language. The teacher does have techniques available for using the foreign language to teach the meaning of language, and these will be very valuable to him on occasions. He can use definitions, exemplifications, paraphrases, in general the verbal context, to make meaning clear. He may also make such relations as antonymy and synonymy quite explicit, although in doing so he does little more than reveal a fraction of the associations into which the form enters. However, these aspects of linguistic meaning must essentially be learned rather than taught, and for them to be learned the widest possible exposure to the language must be provided. As was argued earlier, this is most readily done through extensive reading and can scarcely be done at all if reading is relegated to the position of a minor learning activity.

Mention was made above of translation. Translation is a useful device for providing an immediate interpretation of a new linguistic form. However, since the meaning of an item is the product of relations within the language in which it occurs, and since translation associates the item with a different language, it cannot be said in itself to teach meaning. There are quite a number of occasions in language teaching where we intend only that a form should be understood in the context in which it has occurred. In this case translation will be much the most straightforward pedagogic device to use, but of course we cannot then claim that, because the learner can interpret the form in that context, he knows the meaning of the word. In fact one can question whether one can ever 'know the meaning of a word', since further experience of its use will always add something more to its meaning. This is particularly the case if we consider the polysemic nature of many lexical items. Translation tends to conceal polysemy, by encouraging reliance on one-for-one equivalences between languages. The short-term advantages of translation have to be weighed against longer-term problems that dependence on translation may cause.

This raises the question of the general place of the mother-tongue in foreign-language teaching. There is no need to insist on the total banishment of all use of the mother-tongue from the classroom. As well as the use mentioned in the last paragraph, there are occasions, even in the initial teaching of meaning itself, when we will want to use translation, perhaps because the use of the linguistic and non-linguistic context of the target language will lead to confusion and ambiguity. Translation may also be used for quick and informal checks on comprehension. Where it is important that explanations and instructions should be understood quite unambiguously, there is no reason why they should not be given in the mother-tongue. In this case, of course, one would insist that once the learners' competence has progressed to a level where the foreign language itself can be understood clearly, there will be no need to use the mother-tongue for this purpose.

One possible use of translation that has been much neglected in recent years is actually in teaching the skill of translation itself. The need for this depends upon our definition of objectives, but there is nothing wrong in admitting the possibility of translation as an objective in language learning. It *is* useful to be able to translate a foreign language, although the preparation of professional translators is a matter for specialized not general language learning. Anyone who has spent some years learning a foreign language should not be surprised if he is occasionally called upon to translate something for someone who has little or no preparation in the language. Translation is a language activity that has to be learned through experience like any other.

In deciding how far we are justified in using the learner's mother-tongue, we must remember that time spent using it is time not spent using the foreign language, and when the learner is so short of contact time anyway we should consider very carefully whether any intended use is really justified. If, as is the major thesis of this book, what is learned is a direct reflection of the nature of the learning activity, the greater the use of the mother-tongue the less will be the learner's practical command of the foreign language.

4.6 Language learning and language use

In comparing language acquisition and language learning, we saw that in the former there is no distinction between language-using activities and language-learning activities. All language activity is language use, but in the process of using the child also learns. In a language-learning situation, however, all language activity is language learning and is distinct from and may never become language using. The learner is well aware that he has been brought together with others for the purpose of learning a language. This is why the claim that some methods are 'natural methods' is spurious. The learner is conscious of the artificiality of any language activity that takes place in the classroom. While there is no advantage in reinforcing this artificiality, we should be prepared to accept it, since learners themselves have relatively little difficulty in doing so. Most of the learning activity that has been discussed so far in this chapter is artificial in this sense. Even much of the free use of language that teachers make provision for—by setting up topics for discussion, for example—retains elements of artificiality. Pupils are expected to express ideas that are not their own and opinions which they may not hold. It may not be the type of discussion that they would hold naturally even in their mother-tongue. In a manner that is quite uncharacteristic of most natural language use, they focus their attention more on the linguistic forms they are trying to use than on the content they are attempting to communicate. If it is well done, it can still be a very valuable language-learning exercise, but it falls short of the language behaviour found in language acquisition.

None the less it is our aim for language learners that they should be able to produce and receive communication in the language, and it would be a major contribution to language learning if we could tap or stimulate the pupils' interest in the communicative activity itself, so that in their desire for successful communication they become largely unaware of the linguistic forms that are being used. In bringing the conditions of language learning closer to the conditions of language acquisition in this way, we would be able to exploit a major form of motivation. Many learners would find language learning a far more rewarding experience than is commonly the case. By definition the language activity would succeed in holding their attention. Again this is by no means always the case with frequently-used language-teaching techniques. But, desirable as such an aim is, is it really attainable? There are a number of possibilities.

One way would be to teach other subjects through the medium of the target language. The pupil's need to acquire the subject-matter, assuming at least some interest on his part in doing this, enforces the use and thereby, as with language acquisition, the learning of the necessary linguistic forms. Such a situation is already characteristic of second-language learning, where all or part of the pupil's education takes place in the second language. In foreign-language situations it tends to occur largely on an experimental basis. Some countries have encouraged the development of bilingual schools and in other cases teachers have been exchanged so that they can teach their own subject in their own language in the foreign country. However, interesting as such developments are, it is not likely that they will make a contribution to foreign-language learning on a wide scale.

More conventional procedures that might be better exploited are the receptive language activities of listening and reading. There is no reason why reading material in a foreign language should not be of intrinsic interest to many learners, provided that what is made available to learners has been chosen with their kinds of interest very much in mind. If there are things that people want to read in their mother-tongue, there ought to be similar things that they would want to read in the foreign language. The same applies to the kinds of things that they habitually enjoy listening to. As far as production is concerned, more use might be made of games requiring the use of language. The introduction of a slight competitive element can cause pupils to forget completely that they are operating in a foreign language. The game becomes the thing, not the language. The pupils become very well motivated towards success in communication and that, after all, is the whole point of language learning. Although we do not yet have adequate means to obtain real communication in language teaching, we should make the most of those techniques that are available to us.

4.7 Envoi

Individuals may vary in motivation but they may vary in many other ways too. In any group of learners we will find differences of intelligence, of degree and type of previous educational experience, of degree and type of language-learning experience, of phonetic ability, of attitude, of social background and, sometimes, of age. Add these and, no doubt, other idiosyncratic factors and the result will be different potentials for language learning, different rates at which language learning will proceed, different expectations of the ultimate achievement and different dispositions towards the process of learning itself. Such heterogeneity is the norm not the exception in language learning, and this fact reinforces the general view that is being expressed in this book.

We must adopt an approach to language teaching that is sufficiently rich in the variety of devices that it exploits for the learner to have the freedom to adopt whatever learning strategy suits him best. That is to say, the teaching of languages must be a flexible process. The adoption of a rigidly-controlled teaching programme, involving the insistence on some methodological devices and the rejection of others, implies a general uniformity in the way in which different individuals learn languages. It takes inadequate account of individual differences and therefore will have the effect of favouring some and disadvantaging others. Predetermined learning sequences cannot take into account the feedback that any teacher will expect to receive from his pupils. This feedback will tell the teacher how successfully learning is proceeding, and in the light of it he will continue or adjust his intended procedures. It would be a rash man who would claim that we know enough about learning to be able to predict exactly the path that learning will follow in any one instance. Yet this is exactly what is implicit in the adoption of a narrow set of principles applied *a priori* in the production of a specific teaching programme. The best we can do is offer a set of very general principles that can be followed even while the teacher is adjusting his approach to meet the conditions imposed by the nature of the learners and his experience of observing them in the process of learning. Bearing this in mind we can see how it is possible for a teacher employing 'good' methods, but applying them inflexibly, without regard for the objectives or the characteristics of his pupils, to be unsuccessful, while the reacher using 'bad' methods, at least from a superficial observation, but sensitive to the learning behaviour of his pupils, can be successful, because what he does falls within the broad principles which have been set out in this chapter.